FROM THE
PAST
TO THE
PRESENT

FROM THE
PAST
TO THE
PRESENT

William J. Hodge

CITI OF
BOOKS

CITIOFBOOKS, INC.
3736 Eubank NE Suite A1
Albuquerque, NM 87111-3579
www. citiofbooks. com

Hotline: 1 (877) 389-2759
Fax: 1 (505) 930-7244

Ordering Information:
Quantity sales. Special discounts are available on quantity purchases by corporations, associations, and others. For details, contact the publisher at the address above.

Printed in the United States of America.

| ISBN-13: | Paperback | 979-8-89391-360-6 |
| | eBook | 979-8-89391-361-3 |

Library of Congress Control Number: 2024920060

I dedicate this book to the most beautiful person that I have ever known, my wife for fifty one years. I love you, Beulah. To our five children—Patricia, Aaron, David, Clifford, and Gloria—and also to the grandchildren and great-grandchildren and our fifteenth grandchild, Christian Taylor Barker., I love you, guys.

To all the military families and single military members some of you have and are experiencing some of the same experiences my family and I experienced when I was on active duty. Some of you are going through the same experiences now, such as family separations, not enough money from payday to payday, PCS moves, TDYs, being placed in harm's way. Adjusting to different cultures anywhere in the world in a moment's notice. Getting reacquainted with the family after PCS separations. Working part-time to earn extra money to pay bills. We have learned to survive in any condition, any climate, and on small amounts of funds anywhere in the world. I salute you all.

Contents

INTRODUCTION

I was working in a department store in Covington Georgia as a loss prevention officer when I decided to write this book. I knew I had the desire and skill to write a book, but I did not know what kind of book to write. I kicked several ideas around and finally decided to write my autobiography. Sometimes different events that had occurred in my life would come to me early in the morning and at work. I wrote the events down when they came to me on napkins and scratch paper. As the years passed, I continued to write information and placed it in some sequence. Sometimes I would take a break from writing for several weeks, I realize that my life has been interesting, and I want people to read my story.

CHILDHOOD

I was born in a two bedroom house on my grandfather's farm one half mile from the main house. The house did not have an inside bathroom or running water inside. The farmland is located off Highway 58 about twenty miles from Martinsville Virginia in Henry County. The house was heated with a wood heater and a woodstove that my mother used for cooking food.

My brother Howard was born two years after I was born. He had seizures and was given medication to control them. He eventually stopped having the seizures as he grew older. He continues to take medication up to today.

There were wild animals such as squirrels, rabbits, raccoons, possums, foxes, coyotes, snakes, and deer. There were two other buildings on the property with our house. There was a barn that was used to cure tobacco when it was ready for market. The stable was used for storing hay and other food for the farm animals. There was a walnut and a pear tree near the main house. I remember picking pears from the tree and eating them standing under the tree. When the walnuts fell to the ground, I picked them up and cracked them and removed the inside for consumption. There was an open field located about one half mile from the house. Blackberries and strawberries grew on the edge of the field.

My brother Howard and I would pick the berries and eat them while we played in the field. Our mother also picked the berries to make pies and can them for the winter months. My brother and I played the normal games that kids played during that era. We played games such as cowboys and Indians and rode tricycles and wagons.

When I grew older, I made a gravel shooter. It was a green piece of wood shaped into a Y diagram. Two pieces of rubber were connected to each side of the Y diagram. The shoe tongue was placed between the two pieces of rubber and a hole placed in the tongue to make the connection. Small pebbles were placed inside the shoe tongue, and the rubber piece was pulled to release the pebble. There was a spring with running water located across the highway where we used to obtain our drinking water. We carried a water bucket to the spring and used a dipper to remove the water from the spring. When it was time for our mother to wash clothes, we had to make several trips to the spring for water. We Also had an ice box that was used to keep the food cold. The ice man delivered a block of ice each week and placed it into the icebox.

During our playtime Howard and I caught insects and placed them into jars. I remember receiving a red and white tricycle for Christmas. The next Christmas I received a red wagon and a wooden horse.

My grandparents owned a two-story white house that sat about one hundred feet from the highway. Their sons, daughters, and grandchildren lived at their home. Grandmother performed the entire task inside the home. She cooked pinto beans six days per week. I remember following her to the chicken house to retrieve fresh eggs. She would on occasion pluck chickens from the yard and cook them for dinner. She washed all the clothes by hand and boiled water and poured the water into a tin tub. Next she would place a washboard into the tub with the clothes. She used oxford soap on the clothes to remove the dirt from them. Once the soap was placed on the clothes, a wash board was placed in the tub, and the clothes were rubbed on the board. When the clothes had been washed, they were placed in a tub with rinse water. After the clothes were rinsed, they were hung on a clothesline with clothespins.

When the clothes became dry, Grandmother removed the clothes and prepared them to be ironed. She placed several irons on the stove to heat. Once the irons became hot, she sprinkled water on the clothes and began to iron each piece. She also made starch for use on some of the clothes and dipped the clothes into the starch.

Grandfather owned his land, and he was the only black man around that owned property. My father and his family grew all the food required for survival on the farm. The following vegetables were grown on the farm: corn, onions, sweet potatoes, white potatoes, carrots, cabbage, tomatoes, green peas, black-eyed peas, watermelons, cantaloupe, turnips, turnip greens, cucumbers, green beans, squash, and butter beans.

There were animals that were raised for food: pigs, chickens, ducks, cows, and goats. The pigs were grown until November and were slaughtered during that time. They were placed in a long tub of hot water after being slaughtered. A jar top was used to remove the hair from their body. Next, they were attached to wooden poles with their two front legs attached at the top of the poles. The different parts of the body were cut into sections and stored in a smokehouse. The meat was covered with salt and placed into a cloth bag and hung in the smokehouse.

When Grandmother or another family member wanted to use some of the meat from the smokehouse, they would cut a piece of meat from the hanging meat. The meat would remain in the smokehouse until it was all gone. Sometimes a whole pig would be placed in the smokehouse until it was cut into parts for consumption. The meat that bacon was cut from was also in the smokehouse. The same procedure was used to remove the meat from the pig. The smokehouse was a sealed building without windows and a dirt floor, and it was air tight. The only items that were placed in the smokehouse were different type meats. During these times the smokehouse served as a substitute for a refrigerator. Every farmer had a smokehouse to store meats that were taken from the wild. Some meats were also stored there for long periods of time. The meats that were not stored in the icebox were stored in the smokehouse. There were cows that were milked early in the morning each day. The milk was placed in a churn and a wooden stick was pushed down and raised up in the milk. Butter formed in the milk, and a wooden spoon was used to remove it. When the butter was removed, it was placed into a container. The cows were placed in a pasture to eat the wild grass. When they ate wild onions, the onion taste would be in the milk.

Hay was also given to the cows for consumption. The fields where the vegetables were grown were plowed by using mules to pull plows to cultivate the land. Different fields were used to plant different type vegetables. After each season the same vegetable was not planted in the same field each year. The money crop was tobacco, and it was planted early at the beginning of the year. Rows were made in the fields where the tobacco was to be planted. Holes were made in the rows with wooden pegs, and the tobacco plant was placed in each hole. Also a medal planter was used to plant tobacco. The planter had water in one side and the plants were dropped in the other side, the planter was stuck into the row and water came out and a tobacco plant went into the ground. Once the Plants were in the rows and began to grow, weeds also grew in the rows. The weeds had to be removed by using a hoe to remove the weeds. Tobacco worms also appeared on the tobacco leaves, and they ate holes in the leaves. They had to be removed, and pesticides were placed on the tobacco. A flower grew on the plants that had to be removed by hand. Once the leaves grew to a certain size, it was time to remove them.

A wooden slide box with cloth around it was pulled between the rows by a mule. The leaves were removed from the tobacco stalks and placed into the slide. The sack cloth attached to the slide held the tobacco inside the slide. Once the slides were filled with tobacco, they were taken to a holding area where the tobacco was removed and placed on wooden sticks. The tobacco was held to the wooden sticks by string that was wrapped around a handful of tobacco and placed on the sticks. The wooden sticks were supported by wooden horses. When the sticks became full, the tobacco was placed in a wagon and taken to a barn. The tobacco was transported to several barns until they became full. Once the barn became full, a fire was started in the fireplace of each barn. Some of the barns became full before others, because of their size and the amount of tobacco that could be stored for curing. Normally my father or one of my uncles had to stay at the barn over night to ensure that the fire continued to burn throughout the night to cure the tobacco. Once the tobacco was cured, a date was decided upon when to transport the tobacco to an auctioneer to sell. The tobacco was placed on a truck and transported to the auctioneer. Once the tobacco was sold, grandfather divided the money between the family members, which included my father, his brothers, and sisters. He also paid the bills that had been created during the year. There were peach, plumb, and apple orchards on the property. There were also fig and grape vines on the property. The fruit was used for canning and to consume during the winter months. Some of the fruit was also used to make pies. The apples, grapes, and peaches were used to make jelly and apple cider.

Wheat and corn were planted and harvested into flour and corn meal. The corn was also used to feed the animals. When the corn became ripe, it was removed from the stalk, and the silk was removed from the corn ears. The corn was washed and placed in a pan with cooking oil and fried for consumption. The corn was also used to feed the farm animals. There was a blue and gray cast-iron stove that sat in the kitchen that grandmother used to cook the daily meals on. There was always some type of leftover food sitting on the stove from a previous meal. One food that I always looked forward to was Grandmother's biscuits. I have not eaten a biscuit that tasted like her biscuits tasted. There was a long wooden table about ten feet long in the dining room that the entire family used for holidays and on Sundays.

Grandfather was the businessman of the family. He decided when money would be spent and on what it would be used for. He was always serious, and I do not remember him smiling very much; he was always serious. My cousins were afraid of him, but I would walk up to him and talk with him when I was a young child. He was on the jury in Martinsville, Virginia, and was known by the law enforcement officers and judges. This was a position that many other black people did not have during those times. He and grand-mother slept in a room that we called a front room. He would sit in his rocking chair and read the newspaper. Grandmother would sit in her chair and sew different things. He informed my father and uncles when different vegetables should be planted. He also guided the action that would take place on the farm. I was always curious about how he obtained his land during that era.

Schools Attended

I began school at the age of seven. During these times children could not start school until age seven. I attended Irshburg Elementary School. The school was located about twenty miles from our home. The school did not have a cafeteria, and I along with other children carried our lunch to school.

My brother had begun school but could not continue due to seizures. He had to remain at home with our mother. I remember our mother placing a spoon in his mouth during a seizure to prevent him from biting his tongue. Our mother would also rub his face during the seizure. He was placed on medication, and as he grew older, the seizures stopped.

I attended Leatherwood Elementary after we moved. I attended this school through the sixth grade. We relocated to Martinsville, Virginia, and I attended East Martinsville Junior High through the seventh grade. The principal was the teacher, and he was strict and forced each student to learn the material. He taught about the facts of life.

Integration had not occurred, so I attended an all-black school. During my childhood, my father always worked hard to ensure that the family needs were met. My mother always complained to our father about being tired of living in the country. Our father would inform our mother that he could not grow food in the city.

On Sundays all the family members attended Moral Hill Baptist Church. Grandfather and grandmother would sit on the front row, and the other family members sat behind them. They were members of the church and required the other family members to attend.

It was a sad day when grandfather passed away. Our father and his brothers and sisters continued to farm the land for a short period of time. Everything on the farm slowed down when Grandfather passed away. Later when grandmother passed away, the farm life came to an end. Our father had begun to work for a sharecropper who paid him very little money. He also ensured that he gave our father large amounts of vegetables to make up for the difference in money.

We continued to live on the farm until my father and his brothers and sisters decided to sell the land. When the deed to the land was researched, there were taxes owed on the land that had to be paid before the land could be sold. When the land was sold, the money was divided among my father and his brothers and sisters. Our father continued to work for the sharecropper for several years. Our mother continued to complain about living in the country. Our father would always inform her that he grew up in the country and did not want anything to do with the city. Our father was adjusted to growing food instead of buying food from stores. Our mother had traveled to other states and lived in the city and was not satisfied living in the country. She was adjusted to living in the city, and it would give her an opportunity to work and be closer to different types of stores. Our mother realized that if we lived in the city, she would be able to get a bus or taxi to any locations she wanted to visit.

We also had relatives that lived in the city. The majority of our father's family lived in the country in Axton, Virginia, and he did not want to be far from them. Our mother did very little work on the farm during the time we lived in the country. She would on occasions come out and help our father perform different tasks on the farm. Most of the time she would be home and sometimes went to clean houses. I remember my mother going to work on Saturdays when we were home. I would always tell her to bring me a carton of chocolate milk and a honey bun when she returned home.

Places We Lived

The sharecroppers that our father worked for worked him very hard, and he received very little money. We moved to a house not far from the property owned by our father and his family. The house was about one half mile off the paved road on a dirt road. We did not have electricity. I remember some of the windows not having window glass, and the window had to be covered with plastic to prevent the wind and rain from entering the house. We used oil lamps for light at nighttime. We used a wood heater to heat the house and keep warm. There was a fireplace in the living room. The fireplace gave off some heat, but to get the heat, we had to stand close to the fireplace.

Everyone had to take a bath in a foot tub. The water was heated on the stove and poured into the tub. I always looked forward for daylight to appear after using a lamp for light at night. During the winter months, we slept with our clothes on to keep warm. We did not have heat in the house after we went to bed, and the fire went out in the heater. Mother used a wood burning stove in the kitchen to cook our food. Father worked very hard from early in the morning until late after sunset.

I remember a hedge bush located next to the house with a snake wrapped around it. Our mother saw the snake and began to scream. She was shouting for our father to remove the snake and dispose of it. Mother was screaming, and the snake eventually crawled away before father could get to him.

We had a brother that was born in the house, and his name was John Edward Hodge. He suffered from some type of sickness and only lived for a few years. We continued to live there for a few more years, and our mother continued to inform our father that she wanted to move to Martinsville, Virginia. Father would respond by stating that he could not grow food in the city.

Finally, we did move to a different house in another location. We continued to live in the country, and it would be some time before we moved to the city life . Mother continued to inform Father that she wanted to move from the country to the city.

The next house that the family moved into was located in stony mountain and was also in the country. Relatives on our mother's side of the family lived there. The house was located on a dirt road and had a kitchen and two bedrooms. The house did not have windows, and the wind and rain blew into the window openings. The windows had to be covered with plastic to keep the cold wind out and the heat inside the house. Father continued to work for the sharecropper. He also worked for our uncle that lived several miles from our house. The house did not have inside plumbing. Our uncle had a small farm and some livestock and chickens and pigs. He grew different types of vegetables and corn to feed the animals. Mother continued to complain to our father about moving from the country.

Our mother used the wash tub to wash clothes. The water was heated on the woodstove and was poured into the tub with the clothes. A washboard was also placed into the tub, and the clothes were dipped into the water. After the clothes were completely wet, oxford soap was rubbed on the clothes. The clothes were then rubbed on the washboard until all the dirt was removed. After the clothes had been washed, they were placed into another tub of water to rinse. Next, the water was wrung from the clothes by hand, and they were hung on a clothesline made of wire or rope to dry. The clothes were attached to the line by a clothespin. Once the clothes became dry, Mother placed two irons on the woodstove to get hot. Mother made starch to use in some of the clothes. When the irons became hot, Mother used them to iron the clothes. After the clothes were ironed, they were placed in their appropriate places.

I walked about a mile on a dirt road to get the school bus to school. When there was rain, the road became very muddy, and the mud would stick to my shoes. I normally would carry an extra pair of shoes to change into after arriving at the bus stop. The other kids that lived in the area also caught the bus at the same place as I.

Sometimes we assisted my uncle with gathering his crops from the fields. Our mother continued to complain to Father about moving to the city from the country. We gathered wood from the forest to use in the heater and stove. The school that I attended did not have a cafeteria, so I had to carry my lunch to school. We finally moved to another house located on Highway 58, which was about ten miles from Martinsville, Virginia. The house was on a dirt road about a mile off the highway. The house did not have electricity, and we used oil-burning lamps for light. The doors were not sealed very good, and the wind blew into the house. We also had to sleep in our clothes during the winter to keep warm.

Our brother Henry Clay Hodge was born in this house. He was born with a handicap and only lived for a few years. Father continued to work for the sharecropper who worked him very hard and gave him very little pay. Our sister Lillie Jane Hodge was born and only lived for a short time before passing away. Several years later, another brother, Robert Lewis Hodge, was born. The house was in the same condition as the other houses. The house needed repairing and windows installed. I remember my uncle was in the process of digging a basement under his home. We dug the basement out with a pick and removed the dirt with a wheelbarrow. Sometimes I went with our father to the farm and assisted him with the different tasks that he performed.

There was another uncle that was a barber. He usually cut hair on Friday nights and Saturdays. Occasionally I stopped at his home to have him cut my hair. He used manual clippers to cut hair, and when he had completed my haircut, my head would be sore for several days. When my head recovered from the soreness, I would wait several weeks before I returned for another haircut.

Our father continued to work for the share cropper. I completed my school assignment by lamplight. We played outside during such things as shooting marbles, climbing trees, hide and seek, cowboys, and Indians. The gravel shooters were used to shoot at bottles and empty cans.

I remember our father and the sharecropper planting sugarcane in the field below our home. The sugarcane was planted in rows, and once it began to grow, the grass and weeds had to be chopped from the field. Our father used a hoe to chop the grass and weeds from the field. Once the cane grew into stalks, it was time to cut the stalks. Once the stalks were cut, they were placed into a container and moved into a staging area. There was a machine that the stalks were placed into and were pulled through the machine. The machine pressed the molasses from the stalks. The molasses were placed in five-gallon buckets for future use.

Mother spent most of her life as a homemaker. She was home most of the time raising children. I remember as a child growing up sometimes on Saturdays she would go shopping. She would always bring us something from the store. She was the parent that disciplined my brothers and I. She performed all the spanking and correcting my brothers and I. I remember one incident where she instructed my brother and I to perform a task. We did not perform the task, and she picked up a block of wood and threw it at us. She did not make contact, but we got the message. I remember on another occasion I did something that I should not have done, and I began to run from her. She chased me with a branch from a tree and hit me on my back side. That was the last time that any of my brothers ran from her. She was a strong-willed woman that was always doing things to take care of the family.

Mother continued to inform father that she wanted to move to the city and that he needed a job that paid more money. She was always visiting Goodwill stores to obtain clothes for the family. I would not wear the clothes because someone had previously worn them. I remember on one occasion she came home with a pair of shoes for me. I explained to her that I did not want the shoes. That was the last time she offered me anything from the Goodwill store. Our mother always instilled in me to complete high school and not to get any female pregnant until we were married. I never wanted to miss school for any reason. On one occasion Mother asked my brother and I if we wanted another brother or sister. We informed her that we did not want another brother or sister because we knew how much time and cost was involved with raising children.

Several months later our sister Linda Gale Hodge was born, and the year was 1963. We had to get adjusted to having a female around because there had only been boys in the family previously. I do not remember our mother being sick except for the common colds and headaches. We assumed that she was healthy until later in life. During the early years a visit to the doctor was not practical unless there was an emergency. When a child was born in the family, a midwife came to the home and delivered the baby. My brothers and I were delivered by a midwife.

When my brothers and I became older, our mother began to clean houses to earn money. My mother taught me how to cook because I was the oldest child, and I had to cook for my brothers and sister when our mother was away. Sometimes when Mother did not feel well, I would go into the kitchen and cook and give her a break.

Our brother Wayne K. Hodge was born in 1965. He was a healthy young boy and was very active. During this time very few people owned vehicles. When we required transportation, we called a cab or asked a neighbor to give us a ride. When we lived in the country, it was very expensive to call a cab for transportation. Our mother was easygoing and did not become upset unless someone bothered her children or our father.

The sharecropper that our father worked for used profanity every time he opened his mouth. He came to our home and asked our mother if I could work for him part-time. She informed him that I could work for him when I was not in school and that he could not use profanity when speaking to me.

One day during an occasion when I was working for him, he used profanity when speaking to me, and I left the job and returned home, and never worked for him again. Our father continued to work for him until he began working at the furniture factory.

When we relocated to East Martinsville, I obtained a job working at a restaurant as a janitor. Eventually I was given a job inside washing dishes and making coldslaw and french fries. I was also responsible for checking the food coolers for outdated food and discarding old food. The foods that had a longer shelf life was dated and covered with plastic wrap. I was also responsible for restocking the soda and beer containers at the end of my shift.

Black people and non-Caucasians had to order their food from the back door and take the food to go. Some of the customers that came into the restaurant did not think it was a good idea for me to work in the restaurant. The owner of the restaurant informed me to let him know if I had any problems with any of the customers. I did not experience any problems other than comments and strange looks.

HIGH SCHOOL YEARS

When I entered high school, I was excited and looked forward to the school year. I joined the football team and the choir. I also joined the track team and ran the 440-yard dash. Some of my classmates' parents had money and gave them anything that they wanted. I worked as much as possible so I could purchase things I wanted. My parent could not afford to purchase the things. I also gave mother money each time I received my paycheck from work. The first year of school was used to learn the new information and get to know the new students. My goal was to learn as much as I could. I was concentrating on learning as much as possible because I had a goal to achieve. My goal was to receive my high school diploma in the required time. I met numerous friends in class and others from classes that I was not in.

Some of the classes I was enrolled in were English, history, math, science, physical education, shop, and choir. The teachers ensured that each student learned the information being taught. I looked forward to attending classes and changing rooms to attend different classes. My buddies and I would always check out the young ladies as they passed by.

Since I was working part-time when not at school, I would always purchase my lunch at the school cafeteria during my first year in school. Everyone had their locker, and we normally left our books in the lockers and picked them up between class. I went to practice for the football team and made the team. When the season began, I could only play football at home games because I was in the eighth grade. I worked part-time during the week after practice and continued to be active in sports and school. Some of my friends from junior high school were in some of my classes. There was another friend that lived near the school, and her father owned a dry cleaner.

Evenings that I was not committed to practice after school was used to work so I could earn funds. I continued to be committed to attending classes and obtaining information from each teacher to increase my knowledge.

Football games were played on Friday nights, and we normally went to parties after each game. The cheerleaders and other beautiful ladies would always attend the parties. The night clubs on the block and east end would be jam-packed with people on football nights. The school was an all-black high school. The teachers were all black and were committed and dedicated to ensuring that each student learned the information being taught to prepare them for the future. I worked during the summer months at the restaurant to earn money. I began working performing tasks such as cleaning the bathrooms and sweeping the parking lot. The customers parked in the parking lot when they wanted their food delivered to their vehicle.

After working at the restaurant for several months, I went to the golf course on weekends to caddie. My cousins caddied on the weekends, and they trained me on how it was done. Black people and non-Caucasians had to place their food orders from the back door and take their food to go. Some of the customers that came into the restaurant continued to think it was not a good idea, that I was working at the restaurant. I continued to work at the restaurant until I graduated from high school.

I had two close friends that I hung out with, William and John. The father of the two brothers lived in the country, and their mother lived in the city. We rode bicycles or walked about ten miles to get to their father's house. We did most things together such as going to parties and hanging out. I met many friends in my classes and others from classes that I was not in. Some of the teachers ensured that each student learned the information that was taught in the classes. I looked forward to attending classes and changing rooms to attend different classes. Some of my friends and I would hang out in the hallways during the class change. We would always check out the young ladies as they passed.

Since I was working part-time when not at school, I did not carry lunch to school. When visiting different stores that sold food, we could not sit down and eat the food after ordering it. The majority of the employees at the stores did not want to serve anyone outside their race. There were signs at the water fountains and bath rooms that read White only and Colored.

When we rode to the city in Greyhound buses, we had to sit in the back of the bus. There were always pictures of black men hanging from trees in the newspapers. I informed my mother that I could not live in the type of environment that we were living in. I decided that once I became an adult I would move away from that place and search for a place that my people were treated right. I did not know it at that time, but my people were treated the same way everywhere because of their skin color.

I became adjusted to high school in the eighth grade. I normally would date young ladies in a higher grade than I. I preferred to date older females than the younger females. I enjoyed playing sports and staying busy. I was big for my age and went to the local clubs on weekends. My two friends William and John and I would attend the clubs together.

Finally I came to the end of my eight grade year, and school ended. Everyone was out for the summer, and I looked forward to the break. I used the summer working at the restaurant to earn money. I also visited relatives that lived in the country. My friends and I did not have driver's license, so we walked or rode bicycles. Sometimes we would also get a ride on the bus. Finally the summer was about over, and the school year was about to begin again. Football practice was given in the mornings and sometimes in the afternoon. Everyone was out of shape, and the coaches ensured that they put us through hard, demanding exercises. Finally, the summer was over, and the school year was about to begin.

My freshman year was exciting, and I enrolled in the required classes required for that year. I was also excited to see what students would be in my classes. The teachers were good and demanding and pushed the students to learn the school material. Each class was important to me, and I obtained as much information from the teachers as possible. The classes were exciting, and I continued to have fun. I continued to stay busy with classes and the part-time job. I worked to be able to purchase clothes and pay for school items. I attended classes 99 percent of the time. I did not miss classes because I had a goal to reach. The only time I missed classes was when I was ill with the flu. I concentrated on each class and attempted to complete all homework assignments in the required time. This was the year that I could play football at away games.

A normal day began for me when I awoke at six in the morning. When I awoke I would take a bath and have cereal for breakfast. I reviewed all homework that was due and made corrections to the pages that required corrections. Next, I would get dressed and tell my mother goodbye and leave home to get the bus to school. My father would leave for work before I arose each morning. I would normally arrive at school before the school bell rang, and several friends would be there. We discussed our weekend experiences and the upcoming events at school for the week. I always ensured that I was in class before the teachers arrived. I did not want to be late for classes.

The first class began at 8:00 a.m. Once the first class ended, if there was time before my next class began, we would stop at the lockers and talk. I would always check the time on my watch to ensure that I would not be late for class. After completing the first part of the day, it was time for lunch. Sometimes I carried my lunch, which included sandwiches and some type of cake or chips. When I did not carry my lunch, I purchased lunch in the cafeteria. We would normally have forty-five minutes for lunch, and we were not allowed to leave the school grounds. After lunch I normally attended choir practice or wood shop. My next class was physical education, which I enjoyed because I played sports and exercised. After physical education I showered and went to the next class. There was a study period between classes that I used to review assignments.

When the school day ended, I attended football practice. During the track season, I attended track practice. I also prepared for and attended track meets at home and away from home. I had a good friend, and we trained together and walked home after training. When I was not at football or track practice, I went to work at the restaurant. I ensured that I studied for upcoming test so I would move to the next grade. The freshman year was exciting and fun because I met new friends and had fun learning new material.

My sophomore year began, and I realized that I was much closer to that magic year of graduation. The year began as an exciting year, and I was excited. I continued to stay involved in school activities. I continued to work part-time and concentrated on my classes. Physical conditioning for track and football took up a large amount of my time. I purchased many things that I required to prevent my parents from spending their money for. My friends and I continued to be noticed by the upper class females, and we were taking our place in school. There were two young ladies that were interested in me. I kept one company on weekends. There were two clubs not far from the school that some of my friends and I visited after games. There was a men's clothing store in the city that sold all the current fashions. I purchased all my clothes from that store. I completed all the class requirements to move to the junior class. My friends and I continued to visit the clubs on weekends.

The clubs were on the city block, and only black patrons visited the clubs. I remember going to the city bus station to purchase hot dogs. They were the best hot dogs in town, and numerous friends went there for hot dogs. My friends and I would occasionally see each other during the summer. We checked to see if everyone passed and was moving to the junior class. The sophomore year ended, and summer vacation arrived.

During the summer I worked at the restaurant to earn money. I continued to stay busy during the summer months and also went to the golf course to caddie on weekends. The summer vacation did not last very long. Before I could relax, football practice was started, and everyone was out of shape and suffered the first two weeks. We began practice by performing exercises two times per day. After two weeks of exercise, we were issued pads. Once the pads were issued, we began to scrimmage by making contact. We also learned the plays during each practice. I played offensive and defensive tackle. I enjoyed playing the game and the practices during the day. The sophomore year came to an end, and all students were given the final test. Everyone passed the test and were moving to the junior class when school resumed. I was busy during the summer months earning money and staying busy.

When school began, we had practice each afternoon after school. I was excited to find out who was in my class. The English teacher was very strict and demanded that everyone carry their own weight in class. There were some students that was serious about classes and some not. I knew what my goal was, and that was to graduate the next year. I ensured that I wore the latest clothes and concentrated on my classes. I had one friend that did not comprehend the assignments, and I assisted him with the work in class and at home. This was the year that each of us would be informed if we had the required amount of credits to graduate from high school during the senior year. This was my prom year, and I was excited about it. I began to think about what I intended to do after high school. Some of my classmates from previous classes were in the same classes as I. I continued to study hard and meet all requirements. I worked hard at school and away from school. I was not planning to attend college, so I only enrolled in general education classes. I ensured that I passed all classes that I was enrolled in. The choir teacher scheduled concerts, and I along with other classmates were required to attend. Normally I went to lunch at school, but this year I began to go off campus to purchase lunch. This experience only occurred on Fridays and not during the week. I continued to concentrate on my homework assignments and class projects. I worked hard to ensure that I received a passing grade on my assignments in class. I carried my school books home at night to study and to complete homework assignments.

When the prom month arrived, everyone was excited. This would be my first prom, and I was more excited than some of the other students. I owned a black suit, white shirt, bowtie, and black shoes. I decided to wear the black suit versus renting a tuxedo. On the night of the prom, a friend picked me up, and we drove to our date's home to get them. We arrived at the school with our beautiful dates, and the other guys were checking them out. We enjoyed the prom and all the events that were scheduled. There was a party scheduled after the prom ended, and we attended the party for several hours. After leaving the party, we stopped for breakfast and drove our date's home. The junior year was slowly coming to an end. I had fun and enjoyed my entire junior year and was looking forward to my senior year.

Each student was studying for the test that was given at the end of the school year. When the test was given, I knew that I would be moving to the senior class the upcoming year. I worked the entire summer earning money to assist my parents and purchase school clothes.

When the senior year began, I was excited and continued my dedication to my studies to ensure that I would graduate. Everyone was interested in finding out which student would be in their class. Several friends from previous classes were in the same classes as I. This was the year those classmates were selected as the best dressed most likely to succeed, most popular, funniest, and most athletic. I ensured that I attended each class every day and concentrated on the homework and assignments. I wore the latest styles in clothing that I purchased from a local clothing store in town. The senior year was fun, and I was preparing for graduation.

During a typical week, my day began at 6:00 a.m. when I awoke and prepared for school. I normally would meet the bus at the bus stop at 7:00 a.m. hours and arrive at school at 7:30 a.m. Classes began at 8:00 a.m. and ended for me at 3:00 p.m. When classes ended, I would attend track practice during track season. I did not play football during the senior year. I also attended choir practice and my part-time job at the restaurant. I passed all classes that I was enrolled in and assisted friends with assignments that required assistance. Everyone was doing different things in their classes, and there were different things to become involved with. I continued to be active in the choir. I continued to enjoy the senior year along with my classmates.

Finally the senior prom was coming up, and everyone was excited and deciding who to ask to the prom. I did not drive, and when the prom arrived, I rode with a friend, and we picked our dates up and arrived at the school with our fabulous dates. We had fun at the prom, and everyone was dressed as sharp as a tack. After the prom, we went to an after party that was held at a hotel. There was an abundance amount of food and drink and music at the party. We stayed there until four in the morning and returned our dates to their residence safely.

I began to think about what I intended to do after high school. I remained on track by studying and working hard at school. I considered going to the special forces in the military. I was not planning to attend college, so I only enrolled in the general studies classes. I ensured that I passed all the classes that I was enrolled in. There were several choir concerts that I was required to attend. Everyone was preparing for the end-of-year test. I continued to concentrate on class assignments and remained active in sports. We were at the top of the ladder where all the lower-class students looked up to and dreamed about getting there. Everyone was busy planning the year for the upcoming events. Some students were planning to attend college and were submitting their paperwork.

There was a store located one block from the school that students went to purchase food and snack. Sometimes during lunch my friends and I would purchase a beer. During the summer months, the beer would smell after we drank it. I attended choir practice after lunch, and some of the choir members would smell the beer and make a remark that someone had been drinking. I did not cut classes during my entire school years until the senior year. When I did cut classes, I was caught by a teacher, and she escorted me to the office. I did not receive any punishment because that was my first time. There were parties after each football game, and everyone attended. I continued to work at the restaurant when not at school activities. The counselors began to notify each student to inform them if they possessed the correct amount of credits to graduate. Everyone that would be graduating began to order class rings, robes, and yearbooks for graduation. I was planning to join the military because I did not prepare for college.

When graduation day arrived, I was excited. The most important thing about graduation was to see my mother sitting in the audience. I was the first person from my family to graduate from high school. When I received my diploma, I walked over to my mother and gave it to her. I said, "Mommy, I made it," and she smiled and hugged me. I informed her that I would not have been there without her pushing me and reminding me how important a high school diploma was.

One week after graduation, I received a phone call from a coach at George Washington Carver High School. He asked me if I was interested in attending college. I informed him that I was interested in attending college but could not afford to attend. He informed me to purchase a bus ticket to Kittrell College in Kittrell, North Carolina, for the following week. I informed my mother and father that I would be attending college. The coach informed me to contact the dean of admission once I arrived at school. My mother did not want to see me leave because I had never been away from home before.

The next week, my parents purchased a bus ticket for me. When I arrived at Kittrell College, I contacted the dean, and he instructed a counselor to give me the admission test. Next, I registered for the upcoming classes and was placed on the work-study program. I was assigned to a dormitory room and issued work uniforms. I began to work in the work-study program when I was not in class. There was a facility manager in charge of all the students on the work-study program. There were two three-story dormitories that other students on work study and I would be renovating. The dormitories had to be ready for the students to move into when school began. I was assigned to a team of five other students also on the work-study program. Some of the team members were sophomores because they had enrolled in school a year prior to some of us. We began the renovation process by removing Sheetrock from walls and ceilings. Once the material was removed, it was thrown outside the dormitory onto the ground into a pile. Some of the walls had to be reinforced because the wood strips that gave support were rotten. Some of the team members were replacing some water pipes that extended through the building. We had to remove all the Sheetrock before we began to place new sheetrock into the building. We had to remove all the support structure before we began to place new Sheetrock into the building. The Sheetrock removal lasted about two weeks before the project was completed.

We began to work in the dormitories each week Mondays through Fridays from 7:00 a.m. to 5:00 p.m. daily.

When we began to install the Sheetrock, two team members picked up a sheet and placed it in place until two other members placed nails in each sheet. The project had to be completed before school began in September. The Sheetrock had to be replaced throughout the building, including the hallways and each room in the dormitory. Once the Sheetrock was nailed on the walls and ceilings, putty was placed over each nailhead. The next step involved placing tape over the putty to cover the nailheads. We had to ensure that each sheet of Sheetrock had a smooth surface prior to spraying. Once the Sheetrock was inspected to ensure that the surfaces were smooth, we used a sprayer to spray each piece of Sheetrock to give it a professional look. The next part of the project required me and the other team members to remove the old toilets throughout the building. Since we did not have experience in performing some of the task, the facilities supervisor or his assistant would instruct us on how to perform the task at hand. Once the commodes were removed, the old seals were removed, and new seals were added. After replacing the seals, we placed the new commodes onto the new seal and connected the commode to the floor with a screw and nut. We connected the water pipes to the commodes next. Once this process was completed, the water was turned on to check for leaks. When we did not discover any leaks, the commodes were ready for use. The next process involved inspecting each sink in the bathrooms. The old sinks were removed from the walls, and new pipes were attached to the sinks. The new sinks were put in place, and the waterlines were connected. The water was turned on to determine if there were leaks. When we did not discover any water leaks under the sinks, we were pleased.

The next process required us to replace broken windows and window frames throughout the building. Some window frames were old and could not be used. The frames were replaced with new frames. The glass was placed in the frames, and putty was placed around the glass to secure it. Some rooms required the floor covering and ceilings to be replaced. The old wood was replaced with new covering. When the new floor boards were nailed to the two by fours, the rooms were given a new look. The water pipes in the buildings were broken and required replacement. The pipes did not have thread on the ends, and we were required to manually thread the pipes before use. The pipes were placed in a stationary vice and a threader was used to thread the pipe. Before the pipes were replaced, the water was turned off, and the old pipe was removed. Once the pipe was removed, the new pipe had a stop-leak substance added to the pipe before connection was made. When all the pipes were connected, the water was turned on, and the pipes were inspected for leaks. When leaks were not discovered, all students working on the project were assigned other jobs. Each door and door frame in the dormitory that was deteriorating were replaced. Door locks were also installed into each new door. When the doors were longer than the frame, the doors were cut down to fit into the frame. Holes had to be cut into each new door and frame to place the doorknob and lock.

The hallways and bathrooms had floor tiles that had to be removed and replaced. Once the floor tiles were removed, the area had to be cleaned. Once the area was cleaned, tar was placed on the floor, and the tile was cut to fit some areas. The tile that did not require cutting was heated with a blowtorch and placed on the floor. Sometimes the tar would appear on the tile after each piece was placed on the floor. We had to use a solution to remove the tar from the tile. Light fixtures throughout the building that was not operational had to be replaced.

The final step to the renovation project was cleaning the building. The floors were swept, mopped, and dusted; and the windows were washed. The rooms were ready for the furniture to be placed in place. Each room was fitted with a set of bunk beds, two nightstands, and two wall lockers. The dormitories were now ready for occupancy. The excess material that was thrown outside the building had to be removed. We loaded the material on to the trucks and hauled the material to a dump site. When school began in September, each student was assigned a room in the dormitory. After I registered for my classes, I was placed on work study and worked when I was not in class. The team that I was assigned to performed all types of repairs, mowed grass, paved streets, replaced roof tiles, doors, and windows. We performed all tasks required to keep the school operational. Each building was heated with a coal furnish. I along with the other team members had to ensure that the furnish always had coal inside to keep the dormitories heated. If the furnish used up all the coal, the fire would go out and the buildings would become cold inside. During the fall months, the campus was covered with leaves, and we raked them up and removed them from the campus.

All my classes were basic college classes and one foreign language. I paid for my classes with the money that I earned from the work-study program. I did not have funds to spend during the majority of the time that I was in school. The school cost took all the work-study money. Sometimes when I was not in class or on work study, I worked in the kitchen. When there was excess food, I would take some food to my room to be consumed later. The work-study program required me to be available seven days per week. The majority of the work that I performed was during Mondays through Fridays. The weekends had small tasks that had to be performed. I met numerous students from other states and some countries. The school campus had a basketball and track team. I decided that I did not want to get involved with sports, but devote my time to my classes. There were several friends from my hometown attending Kittrell College. They lived in a house off campus and attended some of the classes that I attended.

My classes began at 8:00 a.m. on Mondays and normally ended at 3:00 p.m. I also worked part-time at a golf course on weekends serving food. I went to work at 7:00 a.m. and worked for an hour before going to class. My freshman classmates were excited to be in college because we were busy getting into different programs and things on campus. I concentrated on studying and completing my class assignments. My roommate was from North Carolina, and we both were on the work-study program. I met a young lady whose name was Mary, and she worked in the kitchen. We became friends and began to hang out together. We went to games and to some of the places that other couples visited. She lived in North Carolina, and I went to visit her during the summer.

I completed my freshman year and returned to Martinsville to work during the summer months. The Afro hairstyle was in, and I had grown a large Afro. Several of my friends who were attending school also returned to Martinsville during the summer to work. I applied for a position at a textile factory and was hired. My aunt was also employed at the plant. When she saw me and my hairstyle, she asked me why I had all the hair on my head. I explained to her that it was a new hairstyle. I was also working part-time at the restaurant. I worked the entire summer at the plant and hung out with friends when possible.

I returned to Kittrell College for my sophomore year and was excited. The year became very exciting because the freshman were initiated by the sophomores. I arrived a few weeks before school began and to get registered and began my work-study program. I also had met Jackie, who was beginning her first year of school. I began the work-study program before my classes began and was given my schedule. When the school year began, new students were arriving from different states and countries. I joined the Lambda Omega Lambda fraternity. The facility manager planned our daily work schedule, and I was always waiting for him to arrive each morning for work. I ensured that he did not arrive ahead of me. Some of my coworkers were late reporting for their schedule, and he was not happy. I continued to work at school for several months before I decided to return home to work to earn some money. I was tired of being without funds to make purchases and do things. I attended school for several months and decided to return home to work for a short time.

When I had been home for several months, I was reclassified and given a status of 1A. My classification status change made me eligible to be drafted into the military. I did not want to be drafted by the military and land in Vietnam. I spoke with an Air Force recruiter, and he scheduled me to take the entrance test. When the results was sent to the recruiter, he scheduled me for a physical. I was given a bus ticket to Roanoke, Virginia, and I stayed in a hotel overnight and was given the physical the following day. I returned to Martinsville, Virginia, and continued to work. I knew I would hear from the recruiter when he received the results from my physical. After waiting for several weeks, the recruiter contacted me and informed me that I had passed the physical. He also informed me that I was placed on the delayed enlistment program because the military did not have an opening for me at the time. I returned to Martinsville and continued to work for a month before I received an entry date. The recruiter contacted me and stated that I had a date to enter the air force.

I departed Martinsville, Virginia, on May 26, 1969, for Roanoke Virginia, where I was inducted into the military. My mother and father accompanied me to the Greyhound bus station to see me off.

MILITARY YEARS

There were other men at the induction center that had been drafted, and they did not have a choice of what branch of the military they entered. After everyone had been sworn in, we were placed on a bus and driven to the airport and placed on a plane. This was the first time I had flown on an airplane. I sat there looking out the window at the clouds and sky. I could see how small the buildings seemed on the ground. The flight was smooth all the way to San Antonio, Texas. We arrived in San Antonio late at night. I had a smooth, exciting plane ride to Texas.

The military training instructors were known as TIs; they met our bus when we arrived on base. They started screaming at us to get off the bus. They directed us to get off the bus with our suitcases placed on our right. We did not know what the big deal was about getting off the bus. Finally, they said welcome to basic training. The training instructors introduced themselves and informed us how to respond to them and to always answer by ending with "sir." We were marched into the barracks, and everyone was tired. When we arrived at the barracks, the time was approximately three in the morning. We were directed to get in bed because we had a long, demanding day ahead.

The lights came on at approximately 5:00 a.m., and there was loud shouting and yelling from the drill instructors. They were shouting demanding that everyone get out of bed. We only had a small amount of time to make our beds, shower, shave, and clean the bathrooms. We were given instructions on how to accomplish each task. Once the task were completed, we ran down the stairs and lined up in front of the dormitory. We lined up in formations, so we had six squadrons. A squadron leader was selected for each squad. There were six men in each row, and there were five rows. We were marched into the dining facility by the instructors. We had to remain in line and looked straight ahead. Once everyone had been given their food, they went to a table and had to remain standing until everyone arrived at each table. Once everyone was at the tables, everyone sat down to eat. We were given a short time to eat. When the drill instructors decided it was time to leave, we ran outside and lined up in formation.

The next thing we did was march to the barbershop, and everyone received a clean haircut. After each airman received their haircut, they were marched to the supply building and was issued uniforms. Everyone was issued uniforms along with a duffel bag, combat boots, dress shoes, belts, hats, socks, blankets, and pillows. The instructors showed each airman where each uniform and accessories should be placed. We were then marched to the tailoring shop to have the uniforms tailored. The US Air Force name tags were required and sewn on each fatigue shirt and field jacket. We also had a dress uniform that we used to pin on the name tag. When the shirts and pants required alternations, each airman was required to pay for the service. The next stop was at the Base Exchange where each airman purchased the following items: shoe polish, deodorant, toothpaste, toothbrush, soap and dish, toothpaste holder, shoe brush, laundry bag, shaving razor, shaving cream, and hairbrush. Next, we were marched back to the dormitory carrying uniforms and all the accessories. We were instructed by the drill instructors how to fold the clothing items such as socks, handkerchiefs, T-shirts, shorts, bath towels, and wash cloths. Each folded item had to be placed in a specific dresser draw.

Next, we were instructed on how to place the shoes under the beds and the order they should be arranged. We were also instructed on how to make the beds correctly. We were also taken through the barracks and instructed how to clean each area. The bathrooms had to be cleaned, and the toilet seats were placed in the up position. The mirrors had to be cleaned, and the water spots had to be removed. The floors had to be swept and mopped. We received our uniforms, and everyone dressed and was marched to the drill pad. The drill instructors trained and instructed us on different marching commands, military history, and how to march and execute different moves. Each airman was issued booklets that contained different information that each airman was required to learn. We marched everywhere that we had to go.

We attended class where we were instructed on military history. We were required to be in class for so many hours each day. We also performed physical fitness training each day on the drill pad. We were also required to run one and one-half mile in a specified time before we could graduate from basic training. Each airman trained daily and practiced running the mile and a half to get in physical shape. The training also prepared each airman for the mile and a half test that was given at the end of the eight weeks. The majority of the squadron personnel were not in shape. The more we trained, the easier it was to run the mile and a half. There were some airmen assigned to the laundry detail, and they processed the laundry. Each piece of clothing that was washed had each airmen's initial stamped inside the clothing to prevent loss. We were also trained on how to wear the uniform and how to salute officers. We also performed additional details working in the dining facilities. During the weekends the majority of us were free to do anything we desired unless we had previously been assigned to a detail. During the nights before bedtime, we wrote letters to our families and made phone calls also.

There were airmen from different states such as Texas, California, New York, Missouri, and North Carolina. I remember that one of my friends that was from New York had a ring on that he could not remove from his finger. Each time the instructor came near him, he would always remind him about the ring that he could not remove from his finger. When we were in the barracks, the instructor took the airman into a room in the hallway during the times we were lined up in the hall. We heard loud noises coming from the room for about five to seven minutes.

We were required to be in bed no later than nine each night. We were awaken by four each morning to begin the day. When I was assigned to work in the dining facility, I attempted to choose the area to work in because I did not care to work in the pot and pans area. I remember one day I was assigned to the facility and was mopping the floors. Whenever there was an airman that did not complete all the requirements to graduate, they were placed back into the incoming class to start over. The drill instructors stopped each of use and asked questions concerning the military that we were required to know. During the eight weeks of training, we were given tests to determine the career field that we would be assigned to. When the eight weeks ended, we were tested on everything that we were trained on. We also had to complete the mile and one-half in a specified time frame. The practice runs each day prepared us for the test. We were also given orders directing us where we would be assigned after completing basic training.

After graduation, I received orders directing me to Kessler Air Force Base in Mississippi. I would be attending the 702X0 (administrative) career field for twelve weeks. Everyone processed out from the squadron and was transported by planes and buses. I was transported by bus, and the bus stopped in Gulfport, Mississippi, to give everyone a chance to purchase lunch. After lunch, we continued on our journey to Kessler Air Force Base in Mississippi; when we arrived at Kessler Air Force Base, we were assigned to squadrons. The base is located in Biloxi, Mississippi, and there were still signs that read white only and colored in different off-base facilities.

There was an airman from the South working in the squadron that assigned incoming troops to rooms and gave them briefings. I was issued bed linen and assigned to a room in the barracks. I walked around the base after becoming situated in my room. There was a dining facility in the building, and food was served around the clock. I used the weekend to become familiar with the base surroundings.

On Monday morning I went to the orderly room and processed into the squadron. I was issued a meal card that was used in the dining facility to purchase food. I was given a schedule to visit the dental and medical facilities to arrange appointments. I was assigned to the 3381 student squadron. My roommate was a Caucasian guy from North Carolina. We were instructed how our uniforms and other clothing should be placed inside the wall lockers and dresser drawers. We were instructed how to keep the rooms clean and in inspection order each day except weekends. We were issued raincoats that we carried in our backpack to class each day. All airmen were issued backpacks. The backpack contained one uniform, one T-shirt, one pair under shorts, one pair socks, one raincoat, one flashlight, and the school books. I was assigned to the school schedule from 3:00 p.m. to 11:00 p.m.

My school group met in the squadron area and formed into six flights and marched to school. The flights were made up of airmen from different squadrons on base. We also had to keep our shoes lined up in inspection order under our beds. When we marched to school, the sun was shining, and the weather was hot during the summer months. When we returned from school, it was during the night, and all airmen carried their flashlights in their hands. The flashlights were used to identify the marching airmen. On numerous occasions during our march to school, the rain began, and we would be required to stop and put on our raincoats. The instructors instructed us on office administration and typing skills. Each air-man was assigned to an Underwood manual typewriter. Each key had letter identification on the keyboard. We were required to learn the keyboard, and the keys were covered with tape after one week of instructions to make us learn. We were also required to type twenty-five words per minute before we could graduate from school.

I met several airmen that lived in the barracks with me. There were also other friends that lived in different barracks. Each airman was assigned to barracks based on the career field that they were assigned. I met airmen from St. Louis, Connective, New York, Ohio, and North Carolina. Many of the people that lived in Mississippi were not for integration. There was a school across the street from the base that flew the Confederate flag each day. The first sergeant for the squadron was from the South, and he had a deep Southern drawl.

We visited some of the off-base clubs on weekends. Some of the people there did not like us because we were black and in the military. There were some clubs that we visited but were not welcomed. We visited those clubs because we knew the good old boys were there, and they did not want us in the clubs. I had a goal to complete school and get out of Mississippi and never return again. There were some good old boys that drove around in pickup trucks that attempted to scare minorities that they observed walking on the streets. We confronted them on several occasions, and they drove away once they realized that we were not going to run away.

The school classes were interesting, and I was excited about learning the new material. We were given tests to determine how much information we had retained each week. We were required to score 70 percent on the final test to graduate. A normal day during the week involved getting up, taking a shower, having breakfast, and going to appointments. The next step involved going to lunch and returning to my room to ensure that the uniform was ready for the day, and in inspection order. The next step involved getting dressed and meeting the airmen in the squadron. Next, everyone lined up and got into their squadrons for the march to school. When the classes ended, we lined up in formation for the march to the barracks. Each airman removed their flashlight from the backpack and turned the light on so they could be seen by vehicle drivers. I would normally have dinner at the dining facility before retiring for the night. This was my normal routine Mondays through Fridays.

Friday and Saturday nights, we would hang out at the clubs. During the weekdays, we had some mandatory formations that we were required to attend. I located a barbershop in Biloxi that I visited to have my hair cut. Everything was going along smoothly until one afternoon at approximately five, the sky turned black, and the wind began to blow very hard. We received a hurricane warning and were instructed to remain inside in the barracks. The daylight had changed into nightlight. Windows were being blown out, and the wind was making a howling sound. We moved into the hallway because the wind was blowing the windows out in the rooms. The rain was blowing under the doors. We remained in the hallways until the following morning.

We discovered that Hurricane Camille had come through the area with 240 miles per hour winds. There also was a twenty-four feet tidal wave during the night. The majority of the businesses and homes had been destroyed. We did not know about all the destruction until the following morning. All military personnel were placed on alert and assigned to assist the civilian community. Hurricane Camille was the third and strongest tropical cyclone and second hurricane during the 1969 Atlantic hurricane season. It was the second of three catastrophic category 5 hurricanes to make landfall in the United States during the twentieth century (the others being 1935's Labor Day hurricane and 1922's Hurricane Andrew), which made landfall near the mouth of the Mississippi River on the night of August 17.

Camille and unofficially the Labor Day hurricane were the only Atlantic hurricanes to exhibit recorded sustained wind speeds of at least 190 miles per hour. Camille killed 259 people and caused $1.42 billion in damages. I was initially assigned to a building to issue food to people when they came for assistance. The city was placed under curfew to prevent people from stealing items from the homes and businesses. I worked there for a few days assisting the people. I was moved to a church along with several other airmen to issue food to the people. We worked at the church for some time before returning to the squadron. The schools had been closed due to the hurricane damage. The school was closed for several weeks. Once the school reopened, we resumed our routine of attending classes. I was looking forward to completing the classes so I could find out where my first duty assignment would be. Each airman completed an assignment form requesting where they wanted to be assigned after completing school.

Finally, the day arrived, and we were given our final test, and everyone graduated. I received orders that indicated that I was going to Travis Air Force Base in California. I had always dreamed about going to California. My classmates received their orders, and they were excited to be leaving Mississippi. Everybody processed out from the squadron and were on their way. I went to Martinsville, Virginia, for a few weeks to visit my parents before going to California.

When I arrived at Travis Air Force Base, I was promoted to airman first class. I was assigned to the Sixtieth Air Base Group. I processed into the squadron and was assigned to a room in the barracks. I was assigned to a room with another airman because I did not have a high rank to authorize me to have a room alone. After processing into the squadron, I went to my duty section to meet my supervisor and coworkers. I was assigned to the forms section with another airman. My supervisor was a black technical sergeant. He was a good guy, and he explained everything in detail. My coworker was from New York, and he was anxious to get back to the city. Every organization on base had a forms account with the Publications Distribution Organization (PDO).

Each squadron representative submitted their requirements to our office on a monthly basis, and we gave them the forms they requested. I worked a five-day workweek from 7:30 a.m. to 3:30 p.m. Monday through Friday. When I completed technical school, I was awarded a 3 skill level. I was now required to obtain a 5 skill level. I was placed on upgrade training to obtain the 5 skill level. There was a training Noncommissioned Officer (NCO) assigned to the squadron that placed everyone in upgrade training in his training program. Each supervisor was responsible for assisting and ensuring that all newly assigned airmen complete their upgrade training. I worked on my training material several days per week. I normally worked on the training material in the barracks after work. I received approximately $100 per month from the military. When not working, I normally hung out with friends and went to the 21 Club on weekends. During the weekdays, I worked on the career development course to complete my upgrade training one hour per day at work.

This was my first time being in California, and I was excited and looked forward to visiting different cities in the state. I knew how to drive a vehicle, but I did not have a driver's license. I had learned how to drive a tractor during my time at Kittrell College. The most important issue I had was to complete the upgrade training. I finally completed all the training with some failures. I now had some free time to do other things. The knowledge that I acquired in technical school was being used at my duty station.

I was issued a meal card when I processed into the squadron. I went to the dining facility to purchase breakfast, lunch, and dinner. There was a wash house in the barracks, and I normally washed my clothes on weekends. During specific times of each month, the customers submitted their forms and publication requirements to the office. I was responsible for pulling the forms for each account. The other airman also pulled forms for the accounts. Normally after each day, I went to the barracks after work and changed. When I was low on funds, I would visit the dining facility at approximately five o'clock for dinner. Sometimes I visited friends that lived in the barracks.

Fridays and Saturdays were club nights for most of us. I did not have a vehicle, so I rode the bus or caught a ride with a friend when traveling off base. I normally remained on base during the week unless I was visiting the men's clothing store in the city. Sometimes my friends and I played basketball after work. I searched for different things to do to keep busy and did not cause me to spend money. The time for my performance report was due, and my supervisor wrote the following comments and was indorsed by the indorsing official:

> *Facts and specific achievements.* A1C Hodge has during this entire reporting period been an outstanding asset to The Forms Distribution Section. He arrived at a time when the forms section was in particular need of administrative personnel. As a recent Technical School graduate, A1C Hodge demonstrated an exceptional eagerness to put his acquired knowledge to work. He presented constructive ideas to improve the forms distribution, one of which was the redistribution of the Primary Stock Order of forms to facilitate easier and quicker locating of forms.

Strengths. Airman Hodge's devotion to duty, military bearing and mature attitude toward his duties and responsibilities are his most notable strengths. His day-to-day attitude is an inspiration to his coworkers. The office has received numerous favorable comments concerning Airman Hodge. He is extremely helpful to the many customers serviced daily by the office.

Educational and training accomplishments. Airman Hodge successfully completed (OJT) On the Job Training for the award of PAFSC 70250A. This usually normal accomplishment is mentioned here because of the requirement that he be able to type in excess of 45 words per minute, a requirement that is definitely not a part of his day-to-day assigned duties.

Other comments. A1C Hodge displayed a degree of professionalism seldom seen in a young Airman. He is highly recommended to be considered for promotion to Sergeant in advance of his entire fellow airman.

WHEN I MET MY WIFE

I remember one Saturday morning I decided to go to the post office on base to visit a friend that was working there. When I arrived, Alex was placing mail in the mailboxes, and I assisted him. After we put up all the mail, Alex asked me if I was interested in riding to Oakland, California, to visit a friend. I decided to go, and when we arrived, we stopped at his girlfriend's friend Beulah's house.

Her name is Beulah, and she would become my wife three years later. Alex introduced me to her, and he went to visit his girlfriend, Polly. I remember wearing blue jeans, sneakers without socks, and a knit shirt. Beulah had cooked dinner and asked if I wanted to eat. I ate dinner, and Alex came back later to pick me up.

Beulah had been married previously and had four children. She was preparing for a trip to Hawaii. I informed her that I would call her when she returned home. Several weeks later, she returned, and I called and went to visit her. We began to date and enjoyed being together. I met her brother and gave him a nickname, Uncle Bond. Beulah and I went everywhere together and took the kids to the movies, state fair, grocery shopping, zoo, and the record stores. On Friday nights, we went to the 21 Club at Travis Air Force Base. Polly, Alex's girlfriend, also went with us to the club. I did not have a driver's license, so Beulah drove to the base to pick me up every Friday evenings.

Once I became familiar with the bus schedule, I began to ride the bus to Oakland. There was a bus that transported military members to the Oakland army terminal that were going to Vietnam. I rode the bus from Travis Air Force Base to the Oakland army terminal. Next, I rode the city bus to Beulah's house. I owned two pair pants, two shirts, and one pair of jeans. I carried a blue gym bag that I stored my clothes in when traveling to Oakland. Beulah had friends that lived in Pittsburg, California, and sometimes we all got together at the club. Beulah's friends were dating military personnel from Travis Air Force Base, and we became friends. Some of the friends were always giving house parties, and we attended when appropriate. We also attended the Kool Jazz Festival at the Oakland coliseum. We also attended the Cow Palace when concerts were there. We located several barbecue restaurants in Oakland, and we purchased food from the one that we decided had the best barbecue. There was a restaurant outside the main gate at Travis Air Force Base that we visited to purchase hamburgers, hot link sandwiches, cheeseburgers and french fries.

I received a notification that I had an assignment to Vietnam. I went to the military personnel center and picked up a list of requirements that I had to accomplish before going on the assignment. I went to the hospital and received the required shots. Next, I was scheduled for M-16 and .38 training at the rifle range. I also had to visit the personnel center to designate a beneficiary. I informed Beulah that I had an assignment to Vietnam and would be leaving within several months.

Travis Air Force base is located three miles east of the central business district of Fairfield in Solano county California. The base is named for Brigadier General Robert F. Travis who died in the crash of a B-29 Super fortress while transporting a nuclear weapon. The base is a very large base and on 24 October 1970 the first C-5 Galaxy aircraft arrived on base. The aircraft is capable of carrying any Army equipment.

The Vietnam War was coming to a close, and racial tensions were very high on base.

A riot erupted in May 1971 for four days in the 1300 dormitory complex on base. The cause was over a complaint about noise, and the entire dormitory became involved. Black airmen were fighting against one another. Some of the grievances the black airmen had were unequal pay and leave authorization. The base commander had a human relations council established. The race issue was brought to the forefront throughout the whole air force.

Finally the time arrived for me to outprocess from the squadron. I met Beulah and informed her that I would keep in touch during my overseas assignment. I went to Martinsville, Virginia, to visit my mother and father. I remained there for several weeks and visited relatives. I spoke with Beulah on the phone before I departed Martinsville, Virginia. When it was time to leave, I said goodbye to my parents and family.

I flew to San Francisco, California, to get my flight. Once I arrived there, I boarded my flight for Vietnam. The flight took eighteen hours, and we made one stop in Japan. When the plane landed, I thought we had gone back into time. The buildings were made of wood, and there were screens where windows would normally be. Several buses drove up to the plane and jeeps with M-50-caliber machine guns mounted on the hoods accompanied them. We were instructed by the military personnel in the jeeps to board the buses. We were driven to the in-processing center on base. We were processed into the squadron and all hand-carried records were collected by the military clerk. I was assigned to the 377th Combat Support Group at Tan Son Nhut Air Base Republic Vietnam (RVN) (PACAF). I arrived in Vietnam in December 1970 and was stationed there for twelve months.

There were only two administrative specialists on the plane that arrived on base. I was one of those specialists, and a friend from Florida was also on the plane. I was scheduled to be assigned to a site in the jungle area. The chief of the base personnel office decided to assign me to the base at Tan Son Nhut Air Base. When I processed into the squadron, I was issued a flight vest, M-16, one ammo belt, hard helmet, canteen, web belt, ammo cartridges, ammunition, and bed linen with pillow. I was assigned to a hunch building that had eighteen military personnel assigned. There were nine bunk beds in the building and one television with one refrigerator. Each military member was given a wall locker to place their uniforms in. Each bed had a mosquito net that was connected to the ceiling and covered the beds. There were black and white military members living in the building. Some of the airmen did not get along because of their skin color. When a black person came to the dining hall or into any of the huts, each person acknowledged each other by dapping. This was accomplished by hitting hands together and repeating some words.

Some black airmen grew their hair long and placed stocking caps on their heads at night to pack their hair down. This process caused the hair to be close to the head and within military regulations. Some black airmen and soldiers plaited their hair. The military did not have regulations covering plaits. The hair was a style and a symbol of the black movement. The year was 1970, and black people had only been permitted to vote for six years.

There were demonstrations going on in the United States against the war and unfair treatment of my people. There was a black airman that I knew, and he had a very large Afro hairstyle, and he refused to get a haircut. We informed him to get his hair plaited because his superiors could not determine the hair length. When he had his hair plaited, his supervisor did not say anything about his hairstyle because the air force did not have regulations covering the hairstyle. The black airmen wore black armbands and black wristbands to show unity. I did not believe in treating anyone unfair unless I was treated unfair.

There were clubs off base that were named after each state in the United States. Some club owners and staff catered to white airmen only. There was an alley named Soul Alley that catered to black air-men. Anyone entering Soul Alley who was not black or came without a black person took their life into their own hands. The Alley was a place where there were apartment buildings and merchant stores. When entering the Alley, there was soul music being played at the stores that sold the music. There were restaurants that sold soul food. The people that lived there catered to the black soldiers. We had our hair cut there and received massages. We were treated better by the people there than some of the airmen and soldiers on base and back home. Numerous airmen and soldiers lived in apartments there. We could relax when we went there and feel at home. There were airmen and soldiers that were absent without leave (AWOL) that lived there. There was a 9:00 p.m. curfew off base, and everyone had to be off the streets by that time. Whenever 9:00 p.m. struck, anyone that was not back on base was forced to stay where they were or locate a place to stay overnight.

Once outside the base, there were kids and adults on the street selling drugs. They approached the airmen and soldiers to ask what they wanted to purchase. There were numerous military members that became drug addicts because the drugs were so cheap. My military job involved ensuring that all military personnel's medical, dental, driver's license, pay, and plane tickets were picked up and placed into their folders prior to their departure from Vietnam. I also ensured that each airman hand carried all out processing records to their new duty station. I was also required to ensure that plane reservations were made for each military member departing the base. Prior to the relocation briefing that I gave on the final outprocessing day, each airman was informed what they were required to bring to the briefing. I was also responsible for processing all colonels and generals out from the base. I picked up their records and made the reservations and went to their office and outprocessed them.

Everyone worked six days per week and twelve hours per day. Some days and nights the Viet Cong fired rockets on the base. The rockets would land anywhere on base and destroy anything they hit. There was a landing strip near the buildings we lived in, and sometimes the rockets hit the pad. The sky would light up every night from gunfire. During the daylight hours, the big guns could be heard in the distance. We had to take cover under anything that we could get under during rocket attacks. There were bunkers that were used when there were rocket attacks. The bunkers had to be checked for cobra snakes and rats before entering them. The weather there was in the one-hundredth-degree temperatures most days. During the rainy seasons, the water washed everything away in its path. When I left the base, there were friends that accompanied me sometimes. The reason we traveled in groups was to prevent the cowboys from robbing us. They were Vietnamese that rode bikes and robbed American military members.

The streets off base were always jammed with people riding bicycles and mopeds. The people that were not using this form of transportation were walking and riding vehicles. Some of the people also had animals with them on the streets. It was impossible to walk down the street without walking into another person. The most devastating thing that affected me was to see small children and adults walking on the streets with missing limbs because they had been injured in the war. The Vietnamese police had checkpoints set up on the streets. They were called White Mouse, and they were crooked policemen. They could be paid off by anyone that committed a crime.

When I was not working, my friends and I visited a restaurant off base named the Red Door. The Red Door restaurant was owned by a black American, and he spoke fluent Vietnamese. Different types of food were served at the restaurant along with soul food. Different nationalities of people dined at the restaurant. The restaurant was a place where I enjoyed eating a good meal and could forget about the war. There were so many American military members becoming addicted to drugs that a mandatory drug test was started. The drug test was given to everyone prior to leaving the country. When military members that were not leaving the country constantly scratched their face and had the shakes, they were also given a drug test. The drugs used by the military members were heroin and marijuana. I was administered the drug test once per month due to the job that I performed. Some Americans went absent without leave (AWOL) because they were against the war.

The major news networks announced the number of Americans that were killed each day. I wrote and called my mother weekly to inform her that I was okay. I also called Beulah to inform her that I was okay. When I was not working, I would normally be in the hut. My coworkers would be playing cards and dominos to pass the time. There was only one television station, Armed Forces Television Vietnam (AFTV). I watched the television sometimes to pass the time when I was in the hut. We played basketball and cards to pass time. There was an airmen's club on base that offered different forms of entertainment for the military and other government workers. I along with other military members felt that the American government was only involved in the war because of politics and money. We did not think that the government cared about the prisoners of war (POWs) or the number of military members that were killed every day. Every military member was given a seven-day rest and relaxation (R&R) anywhere in the world.

Tan Son Nut Air Base was a Republic of Vietnam Air Force (VNAF). It was located near the city of Saigon in southern Vietnam. The United States used it as a major base during the Vietnam War (1959-1975), stationing Army, Air Force, Navy and Marine units there. Tan Son Nhut airport was built by the French in the 1920s when the French colonial government of Indochina constructed a small unpaved airport, known as Tan Son Nhut airfield in the village of Tan Son Nhut to serve as Saigon's commercial airport. Flights to and from France, as well as Within south East Asia were available prior to World War II. During World War II, the Imperial Japanese army used Tan Son Nhut as a transport base, when Japan surrendered in August 1945 The French air force a contingent of 150 troops into Tan Son Nut. By 1960 Tan Son Nhut air Base was growing with more and more VNAF aircraft arriving from the United States such as North American T-6 Texan, Douglas A-1 Sky raiders, Cessna L-19 (0-1) Bird Dogs and Sikorsky H-19 helicopters. (Internet-en.wikipedia.org/wiki/Tan_Son_Nhut_Air_Base)

My friend Myron Webb was in Bangkok, Thailand, awaiting for papers to be completed from the

Thai government. Once the papers were completed, Webb and his future wife would be married and go to the States. I carried some paperwork to him, and several weeks later he received the papers from the government, and they were married and went to the States. When I departed Vietnam for Bangkok, Thailand, I met Myron and his future wife. I was there for one week for rest and relaxation. I lived in a hotel with running water and a bathtub. I did not have that type luxury in Vietnam. I went to the beach and purchased some items that I could not buy in Vietnam. During my time at the beach, I just sat in a beach chair and watched the waves coming in. Myron and his future wife were there also. I went to some of the stores in Bangkok and purchased some items. We went to different restaurants to eat during the evenings. Later after dinner we checked the different clubs out. Finally, it was time for me to return to Vietnam. I said goodbye to Myron and his future wife and flew back to Vietnam.

Vietnam was a poor country, and the people there were doing different things to earn a living. There were clothing shops that sold inexpensive items. I would locate an item in a magazine from the States and carry it to the store merchant. The merchant would take my measurements and make the item I requested. From that point on, I did not need another measurement when I wanted a different piece of clothing. The clothing items were tailor-made to fit me. When I wanted shoes, I would enter the merchant's shop and place my feet on a sheet of paper. The merchant would draw a diagram of my feet and measure across the top portion of my feet. He would then make the shoes from the picture I had given him, using the measurements he had. The store merchants knew that Americans wore good clothes, and they wanted to be in style when they returned to the States. They did everything to ensure that we were satisfied with the merchandise that we purchased.

There was a foul smell that was present when walking the streets. I had never experienced that type of smell during my entire life. There was garbage on the streets, and the streams of water were black from sewage and other things. I could not remember a moment of silence during my tour in Vietnam. My wartime AFSC was performed as an augmenter for the US Air Force Security Forces. I was placed on the base perimeter at night protecting the base with an M-16 rifle. During the night it was so dark that I could not see my hand when I held it up before my face.

I remember one particular night I was on guard duty, and a Vietnamese guy rode up to my post and did not identify himself. I had my weapon aimed at him and was ready to fire before he began to scream to identify himself. Being out there at night we also had to be concerned about the Viet Cong and snakes. I was on the perimeter for twelve hours and could not smoke cigarettes because the enemy would see the fire. Everyone had to remain awake and alert when they were on the perimeter. When anyone was discovered sleeping on post, they received disciplinary action. There was another post in the same area that I was, but I could not talk to the other airman. When my twelve-hour shift ended, I was happy to return to my hut. We had a maid that washed all the military members' clothing. The maid that worked in my hut had to keep clothing separated for eighteen different airmen. She accomplished this by placing each military member's initial inside their clothing. She was paid by each military member every two weeks with Vietnamese money. She did an excellent job washing and ironing the clothing and keeping track of all clothing items. We also had to purchase the detergent and starch for the maid to use in the clothing. Every time I left the base, there was always the possibility that I would not return. I always followed the military directions and observed who was around me. I decided that I would depart Vietnam the same way that I arrived there. I walked off the airplane when I arrived in Vietnam, and I decided that I would walk back on the plane when I departed. Every military member had a short-timer's calendar on their desk or in the hut. The calendar was for twelve months, and the military members marked each day off and showed the number of days the member had remaining in Vietnam. Every military member looked forward to going home. The military members that had a drug problem received treatment when they turned themselves in. If they had a positive drug test unannounced, they would be disciplined and possibly discharged.

Finally I was getting short, and it would be time for me to return home to the United States. I informed the clothing merchants to make a numerous amount of leather coats, shirts, sweaters, jump-suits, and shoes before I returned home to the United States. When the merchants completed making the merchandise, I had received my orders, and the merchandise was shipped to the United States. One of the generals had asked me where I wanted to go when I returned to the United States. I informed him that I wanted to go to California.

When I received my orders, I was going to the 1901st Communication Squadron at Travis Air Force Base California. Before leaving, my friends put together a going-away party for my friend and I. My coworker from Florida and I outprocessed from the squadron. During my twelve months there,

I had been promoted to sergeant. Before I departed from the squadron, my supervisor wrote the following report (my duty title was outprocessing specialist):

> Sergeant Hodge was responsible for the preparation of messages and Air Force Form 330s (Record Transmittal/Request) inquires. He out processed officers and airmen returning to CONUS to New duty status and in country transfers. During the period of report Sergeant Hodge has truly performed all phases of his assigned duties in an outstanding manner. He was responsible for Personally out processing all Colonels and Generals. The perfection of his work and tact and diplomacy resulted in many compliments passed on to the Chief of the Consolidated Base Personnel office from officers. He was responsible for insuring that all sub-records such as medical, dental and drivers records were picked up from each agency and placed in the Relocation folder on all personnel departing for the conus. He was also instrumental in the out processing of approximately 2500 officers and airmen who returned to the conus or transferred to some other bases in the Republic of Vietnam. He is a dedicated Noncommissioned Officer who approaches each personnel problem with extreme devotion to duty. He was a team worker and enjoyed the team environment when solving problems. He displayed outstanding ability to work with others, and had a dependable pleasing personality. He is undoubtedly an airman who should be retained in the United States Air Force and should be promoted ahead of his contemporaries. Recommend promotion to the grade of Staff Sergeant immediately.

The period of this report was served in SEA. After my coworker and I boarded the plane, I went to sleep and did not awake until we landed in Japan. We were only there for a short period of time to refuel the plane. We left Japan and flew to San Francisco, California. I had previously contacted

Beulah and informed her when I would be arriving. She met me at the airport, and I spent some time with her. After a week with her, I went to Martinsville, Virginia, to visit my mother, father, sister, and brothers. I remained in Martinsville, Virginia, for two weeks before returning to California. I also visited other family members and friends during my visit.

After two weeks, I returned to Travis Air Force Base California and processed into the squadron. I was assigned to a room in the barracks. I was also issued a pillow, bed linen, and a blanket. I was assigned to the squadron as the administrative specialist to the communications electronics branch. There were two airmen that I supervised, and they were on upgrade training. I was responsible for giving support to eight subsections. My supervisor was a dedicated individual, and he was interested in his subordinates' success. My work schedule was Mondays to Fridays, and I was off on weekends.

Beulah and I spent time together on the weekends. Sometime we went to the 21 Club for entertainment. Her friend from Oakland would also accompany us to the club. Some of her other friends would also join us at the club. We would normally go to the club at 8:00 p.m. and remain there until the club closed. When the club closed, we went to the terminal and purchased breakfast. After completing breakfast, we would hang out for a few hours before going home.

There were eight subaccounts that required administrative support, and I was responsible for providing that support. The support involved typing correspondence and ordering office supplies for the accounts. I was also responsible for inspecting the accounts to ensure that each was being maintained within air force regulations. I was also responsible for meeting all air force appointments and ensuring that my subordinates did the same. We had a first sergeant who inspected the rooms in the barracks on an unannounced basis.

Beulah became pregnant, and Gloria was born on December 7, 1972. I decided during the pregnancy that I wanted a son. I had purchased a football that I had planned to give to my son when he was born. I did not think about what would happen if a girl was born instead of a son. On the day that Gloria was born, I was in the waiting room, and the doctor called on the phone and informed me that I did not have a son, but I had a beautiful daughter. She had to be placed under a light due to her pigmentation. She also had a gland infection in her neck and was required to have an operation to correct the problem. Beulah was released from the hospital, and Gloria had to remain there for several weeks. When the operation was performed, bandages were placed around her face and head. Weights were placed on her arms to prevent her from removing the bandages. Finally she was released from the hospital, and we picked her up. We were very excited to take her home, and the other kids were waiting to see her.

I went to the commissary every week to purchase baby food and milk for Gloria. I purchased a different type of baby food each time that I visited the commissary. I was living in the barracks at Travis Air Force Base and only saw her on the weekends. Sometimes I went to Oakland to visit Beulah during the week. Once Gloria began to walk, she would come outside to the driveway when I drove in. The kids were excited about having a baby sister.

When Beulah placed clothes in the dryer, Gloria would open it. Gloria removed all the pots and pans from the storage cabinets. Beulah and I had to place locks on all the doors to prevent Gloria from opening the doors. We also had to cover the wall outlets to prevent Gloria from sticking something in the outlet. When Gloria was scheduled for a doctor's appointment, Beulah would dress her and place her in the car seat and strap her in. When they arrived at the doctor's office, Gloria would be undressed and have her hair clips in her hand. Beulah would rush her to the bathroom and attempt to get her clothes and hair in some shape before going in to see the doctor.

During breakfast and dinner, Gloria did not want to eat her food; she wanted to eat the food that we ate. Beulah would always buy expensive dresses for her. When I came to visit on the weekends, Gloria would climb up for me to hold her. Once I picked her up, she would remain in my lap until she went to sleep. The older kids always wanted to hold her and kiss on her. I would tell the kids to kiss their own face and not Gloria's. Beulah would always ask me how they were going to kiss their own face. I was very protective of her, and she knew it. She would only permit certain people to hold her. She played with her toys and took naps during certain times of the day. When we went to the mall or to stores, Gloria would start out walking, and I would end up carrying her. On one occasion she was trick-or-treating, and she went to sleep, and I carried her and the candies home. She was very active from the early mornings until bedtime.

Beulah sent her pictures to numerous family members. We always took pictures of her during the holidays. One weekend Beulah informed me that all the other kids had their fathers at home with them except Gloria. I informed her that she could move to Fairfield, California, and we would be together. I searched for a house and located a three-bedroom home, and we moved to Fairfield, California. Beulah and I had been together for three years, and on October 17, 1973, we were married in Oakland, California. We went to Reno, Nevada, for our honeymoon and enjoyed the shows and sights. The house that we moved into cost $90 per month to rent. We lived in the house until August 1976.

I was nominated for an award at the last base and was presented an Air Force Commendation Medal at commander's call. I received several assignments and refused to accept any of the assignments. I was finally informed by my commander that the next assignment that I received, I would be obligated to accept the assignment. I applied for a base of preference, and several weeks later I received an assignment to Homestead Air Force Base in Florida. I had purchased a Pontiac LeMans six months prior to receiving the assignment. I drove to a mechanical shop and had the vehicle checked for maintenance problems. The vehicle did not require any major work, and I informed the mechanic to perform a tune-up on the vehicle.

After the vehicle was tuned and ready for the drive across the country, we began to clean the house. We threw away a numerous amount of old clothes and furniture. We had purchased a map and planned the drive. We purchased a luggage rack and placed it on the top of the vehicle and secured it. I processed out from the squadron and scheduled the furniture for pickup. Once the furniture was picked up, we began to clean the house. We cleaned each room ensuring all marks were removed from the walls. We removed all nails from the walls and filled the nail holes with putty. We cleaned the bathroom and the stove and cabinets in the kitchen. The floors were swept and mopped. The lawn was mowed and edged, and the driveway was cleaned. The keys were returned to the landlord, and he returned our security deposit. The suitcases were packed and placed into the luggage rack. We placed the kids into the vehicle and began our drive to Florida. I was nominated for an award when I left the squadron. We were not in a hurry to arrive in Florida because I had thirty days' leave to take before I had to report.

During our drive across the country, we decided to stop in each state and stay for the night. We stopped in Houston, Texas, to visit Beulah's sister and her family. We remained there for one week before continuing our trip. I had applied for family housing at Homestead Air Force Base prior to departing from Travis Air Force Base. We enjoyed the drive across the country and took pictures as we traveled.

Finally we arrived at Homestead Air Force Base in Florida. I checked in with the housing officer and was informed that we had to wait for thirty days before we could move into base housing. We drove into the city of Homestead, Florida, to search for an apartment. We located a one-bedroom apartment, but the landlord was reluctant to rent the apartment to us. We could not afford to rent a larger apartment and did not want to sign a lease for longer than thirty days. The landlord finally decided to rent the apartment to us, and we signed a contract and moved into the apartment. After the kids were adjusted, we went to the commissary and purchased food. I removed the car top carrier and all the items we used for the trip. We moved into the apartment during the weekend.

On Monday morning, I reported to the Consolidated Base Personnel Office to process into the squadron. My sponsor had been in contact with me prior to our arrival. He came to the processing line and informed me where the office was located. I was assigned to the audiovisual center as the audiovisual administrative specialist. After completing the processing, I reported to my new office. I was introduced to my coworkers and supervisor. I was informed that I would be responsible for administrative support for five separate sections within the audiovisual service center.

I became friends with one of the airmen, and his name was Bill Mose. He invited me to his house for lunch, and I met his wife, Nellie Morise. Bill and I visited the fast-food restaurants for lunch. We cut the coupons from the newspapers and used them to purchase food. We also visited the local bowling alley on base for lunch and bowling.

Prior to the thirty-day period, I received notification that the house on base was ready. I went to the housing office and picked up the keys. After I picked up the keys, I drove to the apartment, and Beulah and I drove to the house to perform an inspection with a housing inspector. When the housing inspection was completed, I accepted the house and signed the papers accepting the house. I contacted the transportation office and set up a date to have the household goods delivered. They were delivered a week later to our home. When the delivery truck arrived, the workers began to unload each item, and I checked off the items on the inventory sheet. Normally the workers completed unloading the truck within six to seven hours. When all the items had been unloaded, Beulah and I checked for missing and broken items. We had to visit the legal office and search through catalogs that contained items similar to our items that were broken and missing. We were required to submit the information along with the price of each item to the legal office. This was the only way we could get reimbursed for the broken, damaged, and missing items.

When we departed from my last base, my supervisor wrote a performance report on me that read as follows:

> Since being assigned to the Communications Electronics Operations Branch, Sergeant Hodge has performed all of his assigned duties in an outstanding manner. Upon his assignment to the branch, Sergeant Hodge was given the task of completely reestablishing the publications and forms requirements for the office plus eight subsections which included the Telephone Operations Section, Mars Station, Crypto Accounting Section, and five communications centers. He accomplished this task in a reasonably short period of time with outstanding results. Sergeant Hodge further screened the publication files for accuracy and currency. He found many outdated publications in files and proceeded to completely revise the files. This was also accomplished in a minimum amount of time with an outstanding finished product. As a first term airman, Sergeant Hodge has a great deal of knowledge of his career field. He is capable of performing his duties with only the bare minimum of supervision. He is thorough in all his undertakings and constantly strives for perfection. He can always be depended upon to complete any given task in the minimum period of time. Sergeant Hodge Reflects only the highest moral standards, and his personal dress and appearance sets an example for others to follow. His personality and diplomacy when dealing with others is a great asset. Sergeant Hodge is capable of greater

responsibilities and has an unlimited potential for advancement in the United States Air Force.

After unpacking everything, we placed all the furniture in place and relaxed. I drove Beulah to meet Nellie Morise on the weekend. They became friends, and Nellie came to visit Beulah each morning. They started shopping at different stores and malls. During the weekends, Billy and Nellie accompanied Beulah and I to some of the clubs in Miami Beach. We would attend the clubs when a famous singer was at one of the clubs. During the era, disco was in style, and everyone was doing the disco dance. We also went to disco clubs where the disco lights were in the floors. The lights would light up and blink when the music was played. Some of the singers and groups were popular, and some became popular later. I was not being paid a large sum of money from the air force. I had to search for part-time employment with other sources. I applied for a part-time job at the Noncommissioned Officers' club. I went for the interview and was hired as a cook and began to train with the head chef. I began to work four to five days per week. Billy also began to work part-time at Sears. Some weekends we visited the club on base for entertainment. I enjoyed my military duties, and I also had a wartime duty that required me to wear a chemical suit and gas mask.

One task that I performed during the wartime duty was recover airplane parts after a plane crash. My wife began to work at a retail store after we had been there for six months. We met different people on base during our visits to different facilities. Myron Webb was also stationed at Homestead, and we had been stationed together in Vietnam. Sometimes Myron and I would go to Miami to attend the dog races. We settled into our home and was very comfortable in the house. When we moved into the three-bedroom home, we applied for a four-bedroom home. We were notified after three months that the four-bedroom home was available. I made arrangements with the transportation office and scheduled the household goods to be packed and picked up.

When we moved, Beulah and I cleaned the house. We washed the walls and floors with ammonia and clorox. We also had to take the stove apart and clean the oven and each burner. The wax on the floors had to be stripped off the floors. The grass was mowed low and edged. After we completed the cleaning process, I contacted the housing office to arrange for an inspection. After the inspection was performed, I returned the keys to the housing office. When the household goods were delivered from the other house, we unpacked all the boxes. Everything was put in place, and each item was checked for damage and breakage. After adjusting in the new home, we began to take the kids to different amusement parks. They were also enrolled in school, and the schools were not far from the house.

Gloria rode her bicycle to school each day and returned home after school. When she arrived at home, her mother and I were at work. She always called me to inform me that she was home. I would instruct her to change her clothes and get her snack from the refrigerator. She would call me a second time to inform me that she could not change her clothes. I would go home and pick her up and carry her to my job. She would remain at work with me until I completed work. When work was completed, we would go home. Once we arrived back at home, Gloria would ride her bicycle outside. Gloria played with Billy and Nellie's son Roderick; he complained when Gloria did not treat him correctly. When Gloria was ready to enter the house, she would leave her bicycle lying outside at any place from the sidewalk to the lawn. Makita and Carmella were also living with us.

Fishing was one of the popular outdoor sports that I enjoyed during in Florida. Several of my coworkers and I would charter a boat and go deep-sea fishing on Saturdays and sometimes on Friday nights. Beulah and I would also go fishing from the shore during the week when we were not busy. I remember catching a four feet hammerhead shark on a Saturday morning, while fishing from a catwalk. When I landed the shark, I walked the shark to the shore. Once I observed the shark for several minutes, I released it into the ocean.

My father-in-law came to Florida to visit us, and he knew people that lived there when he was in Florida years earlier. I drove him around to different locations in the city to visit different people. He stayed with us for two weeks before returning to Arkansas. During his visit, we located his brother David. He lived in Key Largo, Florida, and his family did not know where he lived. Beulah's father had not seen his brother David in years. Once David began to visit us, he continued to visit us every Sunday. My mother-in-law called to check on my father-in-law during his visit. We enjoyed his visit, and he had the opportunity to see his granddaughter. The part-time employment was working out well. I learned everything that I could to be successful. I began to work during the evening shift. I prepared food for each night that I was working. There were food specials offered at the club on different nights. Sometimes Beulah and Nellie would come to the dining room and order the specials. The "two for one steak" night was offered two times per month. The special was offered for the club members and their guests. This event encouraged the club members to visit the club and support the event.

Several friends had received assignments to Turkey, and I laughed at them. I informed them that there was no way that I was going to take an assignment to Turkey. One of my friends that was going informed me not to arrive in Turkey due to the statement I had made. We had been at the base for two and a half years. Three months after the statement that I made about going to Turkey, I received notification that I had an assignment to Turkey. I went to the assignment section at the base personnel center to check on the possibilities of getting out of the assignment. I was informed by the airman at the personnel center that I had two choices concerning the assignment to Turkey: I could accept the assignment to Turkey, or I could get out the air force. I was scheduled to visit a commander at Homestead that was in a similar unit that I was going to in Turkey.

After the visit with the commander, I decided that I would not take the family to Turkey due to the hardships on families that went there. Beulah and I decided that the family would relocate to Fairfield, California, during my assignment to Turkey. I was required to obtain a top-secret clearance with a special background investigation. The paperwork for the clearance was started by airmen at the personnel center. When I received my assignment orders, I scheduled the household goods to be packed and picked up. When the household goods were packed and picked up, they were shipped to California. My hold baggage was packed and picked up and shipped to Turkey.

We moved into the base billeting quarters until we cleaned the house. My wife and I removed the blinds from the windows and placed them into the bathtub to soak. We removed the burners from the stove, and she sprayed the oven with oven cleaner and left the cleaner on the oven for approximately three hours. We washed the walls and removed all marks. The nails were removed, and the holes were filled with putty. The wax was removed from the floors by applying ammonia and mopping it up. The windows throughout the house were washed inside and out. The lawns were mowed and edged to meet inspection requirements. The bathrooms were scrubbed, and the toilets were cleaned, and the blinds were placed on the windows. When Beulah and I had completed the cleaning, I contacted the housing office to schedule an inspection. Once the inspection had been performed and we passed, I returned the keys to the housing office. The housing office staff was responsible for the paperwork. The housing office staff forwarded paperwork to the base finance office so they could reinstate my housing pay into my paycheck. We departed from Homestead Air Force Base after saying goodbye to our friends.

> Homestead Air Force base is located 25 miles south Of Miami Florida in the city of Homestead in Dade county, Florida. The Homestead Army Air Field was activated by the Air Force in September 1942 and used for transport and training. In 1992 a second severe hurricane, Andrew destroyed most of the base. Currently the US Air Force Reserve occupies approximately one third of the base for operations and training. Homestead Air Force Base is flat and the surface drainage is poor. Canals have been constructed throughout Homestead Air Force base. internet en.wikipedia.org/wiki/ Homstead_Air_Force_ Base.

We enjoyed being stationed at Homestead Air Force base. We traveled to numerous locations in short periods of time due to the location. The base offered different programs for military families. There were numerous outdoor activities at the base. We participated in the different programs whenever possible. We drove across country to Fairfield, California. When we arrived in Fairfield, we searched for a home and finally located a three-bedroom house with two baths for a reasonable price. I remained in Fairfield for thirty days before departing for Turkey. My supervisor had written a performance report on me before I departed from Homestead Air Force Base. The report reads as follows:

> Staff Sergeant Hodge's performance has been outstanding. He single handedly accomplished required administrative details for five diverse branches of the Audio Visual Services Center. He performed a myriad of duties and

met all suspense's. Staff Sergeant Hodge assumed a position that had been vacant for several weeks before he arrived; without the benefit of job overlap. He demonstrated exceptional initiative and established efficient office procedures and working relations necessary to accomplish the assigned tasks. Staff Sergeant Hodge was recently selected for and completed the Noncommissioned Officer Leadership School. His selection was based on demonstrated performance and growth potential. Staff Sergeant Hodge is an intelligent and industrious career Noncommissioned Officer who can be relied on to complete any assignment. Exceptionally personable and self-reliant, he has gained the administration and respect of his coworkers. Staff Sergeant Hodge has demonstrated the capability to assume increased responsibility and grade. His career should be closely monitored to ensure that he is assigned duties commensurate with exceptional abilities. He should be allowed to attend the Tactical Air Command Noncommissioned Academy as soon as possible. Staff Sergeant Hodge fully supports the Equal Opportunity Programs.

After being in Fairfield for thirty days I flew from San Francisco California to Istanbul Turkey. The flight was long and tiresome and When I arrived, the city seemed different from any city that I had seen before. The commercial flight could not fly me to my final destination. I was required to fly on a Turkish flight for a short period of time. When I was attempting to board the flight, I had to point to my luggage that was sitting on the ground under the airplane. There was an attendant standing near the luggage and he placed the luggage on the flight. The flight that I was flying on landed in Incirlik Turkey. When I arrived there I boarded a C-130 military aircraft that flew to Izmir, Turkey. When I arrived in Izmir I was met by my sponsor from the squadron. I was driven to the Kordon hotel and I checked into the hotel. I remained in the hotel until I could locate an apartment. I did not feel comfortable walking on different streets at certain times. "Beautiful Izmir" the "Pearl of the Aegean" is Turkey's third largest city and second most

Important port. A city of palm-lined promenades, avenues and green parks set in sweeping Curves along a circular bay. Izmir has an exceptionally mild climate and many fine hotels. The city is a busy commercial and industrial center as well as the gateway to the Aegean Region. The hotel was across the street from the Aegean Sea and I viewed it at night.

After I checked into the Kordon hotel, I went to my squadron to meet the supervisor and coworkers. I was assigned to a special investigative unit and was required to have a special background investigative clearance. When I received notification of the assignment and accepted it, paperwork was generated to get me the required clearance. The paperwork for the clearance had not been completed when I arrived in Izmir. I worked there as an administrative specialist for a short period of time. I could only have access to confidential information because I did not have the required clearance. I was also the first member of the unit that suspects made contact with when they were contacted to come to the office. My coworkers dressed in civilian clothing, and I dressed in my military uniform. The people would not think I was an agent while wearing my uniform.

When not at work, I was out in the area searching for an apartment. There was a list of apartments on a board in the housing office. When an apartment on the list was available, the housing personnel contacted the landlord and made arrangements for it to be showed. They also sent an interpreter if the landlord did not speak English. Some military members rented apartments together to reduce their cost. My supervisor did not want me to rent an apartment with another military member due to the type of job that I performed. Some problems encountered was locating different apartments in a foreign country. The Kordon hotel had a restaurant, and the majority of the military personnel dined there. There was a television room in the hotel where military members and their families came to watch. We did not have a television station in Turkey. Videotaped television programs and movies were sent to the hotel two times per month. There was also an armed forces radio station that everyone listened to. When the Super Bowl came on the radio, I awoke at 2:00 a.m. to listen to the game.

I searched for an apartment for three weeks before I finally located an apartment. The apartment had one bedroom, kitchen, bathroom, and a balcony. The landlord sent a cleaning lady to the apartment to clean it before I moved in. When I met the landlord, she signed the contract, and she informed me when the rent would be due each month. I purchased lunch for the cleaning lady because she continued to work without eating. The Turkish people are Muslims, and the women wore head covers and clothing that covered their entire body. The younger women dressed the same as American women dress. After spending several hours in the apartment, I contacted the housing office and informed the staff to set up a delivery date for a stove and bed to be delivered to my apartment. The stove required a hookup to a gas bottle. I walked down the street to a merchants store and purchased a gas bottle. I also had the gas bottle refilled when it became empty. I also instructed the housing officer to have a refrigerator delivered to my apartment. I could not drink the water from the faucet, so the water had to be boiled or purified before consuming. I also poured two tops of Clorox into a five gallon container of water. The water in the shower was cold, and I did not have hot water unless I heated it on the stove.

When I was in the apartment during the winter months, I would spend most of the time in the kitchen to keep warm. The only place in the apartment with heat was the kitchen. I turned the stove burners and oven on to generate heat in the kitchen. I normally remained in the kitchen on weekends when I was home. During the weekdays when I was home, I turned the burners on until I retired for the night. My bed had an electrical blanket, and I turned the blanket on to keep warm.

There were numerous stores on the streets less than a mile from my apartment. I had visited the stores on numerous occasions. During the mornings when I was walking to work some, of the store owners came out to say hello. One morning I was walking to work, and a merchant came out to say good morning in the Turkish language. I spoke back to him in the Turkish language. There was an American lady walking behind me and going in the same direction. When we arrived at our final destination, she asked me if I was an American. I replied that the last time that I checked, I was an American.

During the winter and rainy season, I rode a taxi to work. There was a taxi driver that picked me up each morning and drove me to work. After being in the squadron for several months, I had not received my security clearance. I was reassigned to the security police squadron as the wing base administrative specialist. I performed all the office administration functions for the squadron. I was responsible for making initial distribution of incoming publications and other types of correspondence. I maintained publication files in a current status by posting newly received publications, supplements, and changes. I also typed drafts, letters, messages, and airmen performance reports.

I remember being in my apartment on a Saturday morning during the winter sitting in the kitchen near the stove. I had turned all the top burners and oven on to warm the kitchen. During the time I was there, I placed my feet on the top of the stove and fell asleep. When I came out of the sleep, I smelled rubber burning. I looked down and noticed that my shoe sole was on fire. I jumped up and began to beat my shoe on the floor to extinguish the flames.

Since my apartment did not have hot water, I went to the gym each day to take a shower. I normally worked out during the times I visited the gym. There was a small commissary located in the city for military and civil service personnel to purchase food and supplies. There was a limit on some food items because the items could be sold on the black market. There were some meat items that could be purchased in the commissary. Each military member and civil servant was issued a ration card upon arrival. When controlled items were purchased in the commissary, they were punched on the card to show purchase. If the member was authorized five cartons of cigarettes per month, five was the magic number that could be purchased. Some items that were not used did not get punched on the ration card.

Turkey is a beautiful country, and people from all over the world go there on vacation. Many of the streets were made with cobblestone. Being in the military in turkey was not always safe for the military member. Some military members did not wear the uniform when walking on the streets. I wore civilian clothing to work and changed into my uniform after arriving at work. I began to work part-time at the hotel to supplement my military check because the checks were sent to the States for my family.

I did not have personal transportation because I left my vehicle for my wife to use. When I wanted to travel, I hired a taxi or rode on the public transportation on Turkish buses. The bus fare was inexpensive, but most Americans did not ride on the bus because it was always full with passengers. I also walked more during my assignment in Turkey than any other assignment. Most of the time I walked to work when the weather was good. The building that I was assigned to have stairs that I walked up several times per day. The apartment building where I lived has six flights of stairs, and I lived on the sixth floor. I walked up six flights each day seven days per week. I received the required amount of exercise each day.

There were only three Airmen in my career field (702X0) assigned to the squadron. During certain times of the year, the orderly room airmen were required to issue some controlled forms at specific times. I volunteered to assist the airmen with issuing the forms to ensure they were issued by the due date. I ensured that all procedures and policies were correct and adhered to. I also purchased some items on the economy that I would ship to the States.

I learned how to say hello and goodbye in the Turkish language. During Saturdays a friend and I visited some stores, and we were given ice cream by the employees. During the summer months numerous airmen enjoyed the walk along the Aegean Sea wall. The Turkish people also walked along the wall. I enjoyed standing on the balcony in the Kordon hotel at night, looking out into the Aegean Sea.

The work in Turkey was done at a slower pace than in the States. When I arrived in Turkey, there was an apartment building under construction across from my apartment building. One year later the building was still being built. The buildings in Turkey were built by hand. The streets were always crowded with people walking and riding bicycles. The vehicle drivers blew their horns when approaching red lights and continued to proceed ahead. I met some good people in Turkey that I call friends. I would love to return to Turkey on vacation. During my tour in Turkey, I was looking forward to returning to the States. I had to return to the States on emergency leave. I had served most of my tour when I had to return to the States. I was reassigned within the United States and did not have to return to Turkey. I processed out of the squadron and gave a friend power of attorney to ship my property to the United States after I departed.

I received notification before my departure that I had been reassigned to Beale Air Force Base. I completed the paperwork for my family to reside on base. I phoned my wife and informed her that we were going to Beale Air Force Base in Yuba City, California. My mother had been suffering from cancer, and I was not aware of her condition until I came home. She had been receiving chemotherapy treatments for the cancer after the discovery.

When I arrived in the States, I went to Martinsville, Virginia, after landing in California to visit her. I stayed at home for several weeks before returning to California. My mother seemed happy, and she was in good spirits during the time I was there. When I arrived in Fairfield, California, I contacted the transportation office and made arrangements to have the household goods packed and shipped to Beale Air Force Base. My wife and I cleaned the house after the household goods were packed and picked up.

When we arrived at Beale Air Force Base, I contacted the housing office for the availability of a house. I was informed by the housing employee that a house was available. I picked up the keys to the house, and my wife and I drove to the house to inspect it. My wife and I decided to accept the house after the walk through. I contacted the transportation office and gave them our new address. I also arranged to have the household goods delivered to our home. The household goods were delivered to our residence within two days. When the household goods were delivered and unpacked, we had to go through the process of identifying broken items. We also had to check the inventory list for missing items. We also had to go to the legal office to file a claim. When the claim was filed, we went to the Base Exchange to locate similar items in the catalogue. After filing the claim, we received a check in the mail within three to four weeks.

When I departed from my last duty station, my supervisor wrote a performance report on Me. The report was written as follows:

> Staff Sergeant Hodge is truly an outstanding Non commissioned Officer. He was the only Administrative Specialist assigned to support a sixty man Security Police element. He was able to give professional guidance and support to all personnel. Upon assuming his duties he had to completely revise and update the administrative process and procedures. His outstanding ability enabled him to complete an average of twenty letters a week for command element signatures. Recognizing that the unit maintained an excessive number of forms and publications, Staff Sergeant Hodge systematically screened and reduced the overall account by approximately thirty percent. He continued to plan and program all security police files and correspondence in an extremely professional manner. His knowledge of the Air Force administrative policies and procedures is extremely noteworthy. On occasion he has

been able to assist other administrative specialists assigned to the detachment. When the detachment contracting office and the squadron orderly room had an excessive amount of typing to be accomplished, he volunteered to assist. This typing support has enabled the contracting office to process and expedite last minute purchase requests.

The orderly room personnel had to issue unit ration cards by the required suspense date and maintain their normal work requirements. Staff Sergeant Hodge maintains the skill, initiative and professional qualities to be given increased duties and responsibilities. He strongly believes in and supports the Equal Opportunity Program. This report covered the period of 1 March 1979 to 29 February 1980.

I went to the squadron and processed in and checked with my new supervisor to find out where I would be working. I was assigned to the Intelligence Plans and Programs Division. I was responsible for the accurate completion of numerous messages and reports created by the division. Many times under the pressure of very short suspenses, I completed numerous and diverse administrative tasks. I wrote division operating instructions, which implemented new procedures for processing temporary duty orders. The operating instruction was well organized and clearly presented. I received administrative inspections, which was free of discrepancies. The inspecting officials report commended on the fine manner in which the publications and files were maintained. One of my prime responsibilities was the preparation of officer evaluation reports (OER) and travel orders for the intelligence directorate offices. There was one other Noncommissioned Officer (NCO) that worked in the office. I always ensured that my appearance and uniforms were in the proper order. I would compare my uniform and shoes with the other NCOs many times. I was required to keep my duffel bag packed with uniforms in case I was sent on a temporary duty assignment (TDY).

I was also enrolled in an algebra class, and the operations officer, who was a second lieutenant, assisted me with solving the problems. I came to work each day one hour before work so the lieutenant would be available to help me. I passed the course, and one of the requirements for obtaining my degree was accomplished. I continued to take other classes to reach the goal that I had set. I did not think about going on an assignment because I was happy with my assignment at Beale Air Force Base.

> The host unit at Beale Air Force base is the Reconnaissance Wing (9RW) assigned to the Air Combat Command and part of Twelfth Air Force. The 9RW collects intelligence essential for presidential and congressional decisions critical to the national defense. To accomplish this mission, the wing was equipped with a fleet of U-2 Drago lady RQ-4 Global Hawk unmanned aircraft and the MC-12 Liberty Reconnaissance Aircraft and assorted support equipment. Internet en.wikipedia.org/wiki/Beal Air Force Base.

I worked in a building on base called a block building. The military members working in the building were required to have a security clearance. I enjoyed my job and looked forward to the daily challenges. I worked part-time at the bowling alley on Friday and Saturday nights. I performed janitorial work and cleaned the bowling lanes. I also oiled the lanes after cleaning each lane. I always persuaded my wife to go with me to the bowling alley. I had to wait until twelve midnight to clean. My wife would normally be asleep at that time, and when I would wake her to ask if she was going with me, sometimes she would say she did not know.

We went to Sacramento and Concord, California, to shop at the malls. The city we lived in did not have a mall. We left home early in the morning and would spend the entire day at the mall. We had a very large yard at our home, and we did not own a lawn mower. The onbase housing office had a building with lawn equipment. I borrowed a lawn mower to cut the grass. The mower that I was given did not have a motor. I had to push the mower using muscle power to cut the lawn. When I completed the yard, I used a shovel to edge the yard.

My wife and I went to Rio Vista to fish in the Sacramento River for bass and catfish. We would purchase the bait a day before and store it in the refrigerator until the day we used it. I checked my tackle box to ensure that we had hooks and weights for the trip. On the day of the trip my wife prepared lunch for us to carry on the trip. When we left home, I would stop at a store and purchase ice to keep the food cold. I also used a cooler for storing the fish in that we caught.

When we arrived at the fishing spot, we unloaded the vehicle and placed the fishing chairs out. Sometimes we did not catch any fish, but we relaxed just sitting there watching the waves and ripples in the water. We normally remained on the riverbank for six to eight hours. When we caught fish under the required size, they were returned to the river. There were numerous snags that caught the hooks on occasion that caused my wife and I to lose our weights and hooks. When this happen, I replaced the lose hooks and weights. When hooks and weights are lost, this becomes expensive to replace them. We attempted different procedures to reduce the loss of the weights and hooks.

When I located a fishing rod on sale, I would eventually purchase it. I would always purchase my wife a rod and reel when I purchased one for myself. The only time that my wife did not accompany me fishing was when I went deep-sea fishing. When I went deep-sea fishing, five friends and I would put our money together and charter a boat. We also departed early in the morning and returned late in the afternoon. This is a sport that I enjoyed doing when I could get away. I continue to enjoy this sport to this day.

My wife found a job at the shopette on base after several weeks of seeking employment. She would bring me chips and dip each night when she came home from work. I took care of the kids when she was at work. We visited the bay area when there were entertainers at the cow palace in San Francisco California. I remember that we always attended the Kool Jazz Festival at the Oakland coliseum. I also enjoyed the professional sports events and attended some of the games when time permitted.

My job continued to be challenging and exciting. There were other noncommissioned officers in the unit that were receiving assignments to Offutt Air Force Base in Nebraska. I did not want to go to Offutt Air Force Base, so I decided to apply for an overseas base. I was assigned to the Ninth Strategic Reconnaissance Wing from March 1, 1980, to February 28, 1981. I received an assignment to Spangdahlem Air Base in Germany. My supervisor wrote the following performance report:

> Staff Sergeant Hodge is an outstanding Non commissioned Officer in every respect. His performance of duty epitomizes that of the true Air Force professional. This talented NCO was the mainstay in revitalizing the

Plans and Programs Division Administrative Section. His comprehensive knowledge of complex administrative and special security requirements have enabled him to establish new procedural guidance within the division. His meticulous attention to detail not only enhanced the professional quality of the voluminous message traffic.

His attention to detail ensured all correspondence created by the division was properly Safe guarded. This has been a crucial factor in insuring the proper safeguarding of highly classified material. Because of his superb attitude and plain hard work, he completely rebuilt the division classified and unclassified files. His efforts were culminated when a Headquarters Strategic Air Command (SAC) Operational Readiness Inspection rated the administrative files as "Excellent". Staff Sergeant Hodge's outstanding leadership skills, extensive knowledge, and "can do" attitude make him an invaluable asset to the Air Force. He has established an excellent rapport with all enlisted and officer ranks and his opinions are respected by all. Staff Sergeant Hodge completed a Management Science Course from Chapman College and enrolled in a Business Statistic course. I highly recommend promotion well in advance of his contemporaries.

I was contacted by the American Red Cross that my mother had passed away. This was one of the most devastating things that I had ever experienced in my life. I made arrangements and caught a flight from California to North Carolina. When I arrived in Martinsville, Virginia, my father and brother had made all the funeral arrangements. I had always remembered other people at funerals and their reactions after losing a family member. Now I would go through the same experience as the other people had gone through. I ensured that each family member had the proper clothing to wear to the funeral. Family members and friends came to our house to give their condolence; on the day of the funeral when we arrived at the church, we stood outside for a while before entering. I was remembering that I had never seen my mother sick. I only remember her having colds, toothaches, and headaches. I always thought my parents would live forever.

When we entered the church, I saw friends and family members that I had not seen for years. I was seated next to my father followed by my brothers and sister. After the service, we left the church and drove to the cemetery to bury our mother. Some family members and friends attended the burial ceremony. We returned home and family members and friends came to the house to give our father their condolence. I remained at home for a week after the funeral to assist my father with the removal of mother's items from the home. The only items left in the house were the things our father wanted to remain there. There was a sofa that our mother slept on in the living room when she was alive. My sister Linda and brother Keith were afraid to lie on the couch at night. I slept on the couch to show them that there was nothing to be afraid of.

After being at home for a while, I returned to California to be with my family. I had received an assignment to Spangdahlem Air Base in Germany. I was required to report in September 1981. My mother had been gone for twenty years, and I continued to think about her. I guess when you lose a loved one, you always remember them for the rest of your life.

Beulah wanted to remain in the States so she could be near the oldest kids. I outprocessed from the squadron and picked up my tickets and other required paperwork. We located a house in Fairfield, California, for Beulah and the kids to live. I made the arrangements to have the household goods picked up. They were packed and shipped to the new address in Fairfield. I also had the items I was shipping to Germany picked up and shipped. Beulah and I cleaned the house on base and prepared it for inspection by the housing personnel. All military members had to ensure that everything was cleaned prior to returning the house keys to the housing office. We cleaned the walls and removed all nails and markings. The nail holes were filled with putty. The wax was stripped from the floors with ammonia. Sometimes we used ammonia and Clorox to clean the house. We took the stovetop off and cleaned the burners and oven. The window blinds were removed from each window and taken outside and washed with soap and water. The windows and ledges were cleaned and washed. The bathrooms were cleaned, and the water spots were removed from the walls. The yard was mowed and edged. After all these things were done, a housing officer was contacted to arrange for an inspection of the house. Once the inspection was done, the keys were returned to the housing office. The housing officer contacted the finance office to inform them that we did not live on base anymore. The finance office processed paperwork returning the money for housing to my paycheck.

When the furniture was delivered to the new residence, it was unloaded and placed in each room. My wife and I had cleaned the house and placed curtains on the windows. We rented a carpet shampooer to clean the carpet throughout the house. I did not want to leave the family in the United States while I was in another country. After getting the family settled, Beulah drove me to the San Francisco airport, and I boarded my flight for Germany. I had been in contact with my military sponsor, and he was scheduled to meet me when I arrived in Germany.

The flight was very long, and it took approximately eighteen hours. Everyone on the flight watched movies and were served breakfast, lunch, and dinner. We stood and walked and stretched to pass the time. When the plane finally landed, there were military buses available to transport all military personnel to the different bases and posts. My military sponsor did not meet me in Frankfurt, so I rode a military bus to Spangdahlem Air Base. When I arrived at the base, I was issued bedsheets, blankets, one pillow, and a room in the barracks. I arrived on base during the weekend and had to wait until Monday morning to process into the squadron.

The weather had began to turn cold and was windy. The country was very beautiful, and I was anxious to see it during my tour. It took me several days to adjust to the time difference, and I went to sleep for approximately twelve hours before awaking. When I finally awoke, I was hungry, so I went to the dining facility to eat. The food tasted different than the food that I was familiar with eating. I explored the base over the weekend to become familiar and adjusted to my new surroundings.

On Monday morning I went to the personnel office and the Consolidated Base Personnel Office to process into the squadron. I was scheduled to go to a unit that processed classified material. I could not go to the unit I was assigned because my security clearance paperwork had not been completed. I was reassigned to the Base Supply Squadron as the wing base supply administrative specialist, Material Management Branch. I typed, edited, and dispatched outgoing correspondence after reviewing it for administrative correctness. I complied, typed, and filed special reports as required. I also maintained functional publication sets and emergency forms requirements. I coordinated personnel actions between the unit orderly room and functional area of assignment. I identified special problems and assisted the customer account representative and functional area documentation managers in conducting specialized training for other administrative personnel. I also monitored and administered the unit intro program.

When I arrived in Germany, the housing office had a house available for my family and I to move into. I had to refuse to accept the house because my family was in the United States. I had to reapply for another house for my family when they arrived later. My supervisor wrote the following comments about my performance.

> Staff Sergeant Hodge is an outstanding Administrative Specialist. He has a broad knowledge of his assigned duties and is well versed in other lateral administrative areas. There have been several consolidations, as well as procedural and organizational changes, which have thrown heavy workloads on the squadron administrative section. In every instance, the changes have been made, and work has been accomplished in a timely and efficient manner. Staff Sergeant Hodge's know how and experience also brought outstanding results in the area of publications and forms management. He did this identifying special problems and assisting the Customer Account Representative (CAR) and Functional Area Documentation Manager (FADM) in conducting specialized training for other administrative personnel. Staff Sergeant Hodge's most productive area has been his monitoring and administration of the Unit Intro program. During a five month period thirty-three sponsor packages were compiled and mailed out. One package was noted for a minor error. This achievement is directly attributed to Staff Sergeant Hodge's administrative skills, dedication, and hard work. Staff Sergeant Hodge's full interest and enthusiastic attitude toward mission accomplishment are his main

assets. Staff Sergeant Hodge is striving to complete a Bachelor of Arts degree in management. He successfully completed a course in Resource Management with the University of Maryland. A professional in every sense, his bearing and devotion to duty make him an outstanding Noncommissioned Officer.

I continued to enjoy being in Germany and in the squadron. I also typed and distributed all operational plans outbound by division personnel.

I was responsible for the currency of all plans stored in the division and posted all changes by the effective date. Finally, my security clearance paperwork arrived at the base personnel office. I was notified on a Friday afternoon and had to contact the squadron commander. When I contacted the squadron commander, I informed him about my clearance, and he stated that he would contact my new supervisor and arrange a transfer date. The date was set, and I processed out of the supply squadron and into the Fifty-Second Tactical Fighter Wing Plans Division.

When I arrived at the Plans Division, I met my supervisor who was a Lieutenant Colonel. He explained my job requirements to me and introduced me to the two majors and one captain that was assigned to the office. They were responsible for drafting the plans and finalizing them. I was the top-secret control noncommissioned officer. I controlled and distributed over one hundred NATO and national plans classified through top secret. I was also the administrative support shift supervisor for the wing senior battle staff during exercises and contingency operations. My new office was located underground inside the command post. When entering the building, I had to be buzzed into the building by a control officer. Once inside the building, there was a combination lock on my office door. Once the door was opened and I entered my office, the correspondence that I was responsible for were located in five locked filing cabinets, and each had a combination lock. I typed the plans from a draft and checked for punctuation and correct word spelling. I was also responsible for mailing classified documents and correspondence to other outside agencies. I was also responsible for receiving all classified documents when they arrived. I destroyed all outdated classified documents by burning them. Forms were generated to list the destroyed documents.

I had to adjust to being in the exercises that were given every two months. Everyone participated in the exercises, and no one was exempted. Everyone was required to be in full chemical gear, including gas mask and gloves. The exercises trained and prepared the troops for wartime chemical attacks that could be launched at troops in foreign countries. When the gas masks were first placed on, many military members could not breathe because the mask was not sealed properly. When I first placed the mask on and attempted to breathe, I could not, because the mask was not sealed. After learning how to seal the mask, I could breathe.

During the winter months, the chemical suit kept the body warm. During the summer months, the chemical suit was too hot and caused military personnel to sweat more than they would normally. During some exercises I along with other military members were required to relocate to different buildings. This procedure prepared us to move from one location in case we received chemicals in the location where we were. I do not think everyone enjoyed wearing the chemical suits. Everyone realized that the chemical suit may save their life one day, if worn and used properly. Sometimes we were taken into a gas chamber without the mask on and were instructed after several minutes to place the mask on. If the mask did not seal after placing it on, the gas would continue to burn the eyes and nostrils. I did not look forward to wearing the chemical suit and participating in the exercises. I realized that the training was given to save lives. We were also trained how to administer a shot to ourselves and others if chemicals entered the pores in the skin. During the exercises, each military member had to perform a wartime duty. This was a duty that we would perform in a real war. Each building on the base would have the windows covered.

During exercises simulated explosions occurred outside and inside the building. When the explosions occurred inside the buildings, there were evaluators that would be present, and they would direct the military members to evacuate from the building or die. When the explosion occurred outside the buildings and military members were walking, they had to take cover in ditches or any place available that could shield them from the explosion. There were medical military members that treated the wounded, and they were transported to the medical facility.

We could not attend the dining facility during the exercises, so we ate the meals provided to us. These meals were meals ready to eat (MREs). Some of the foods were inside cans and the others were in different containers. Some of the food required water to be added, and it was ready for consumption. I along with other military members also prepared food to bring if we did not want to eat the meals ready to eat. Each one of us were placed on shifts, and we were not permitted to leave the location once the exercise began. We were evaluated by military inspectors on how we performed under pressure during different circumstances. Everyone looked forward to the ending day of the exercise. We knew the next day after the exercise ended, everything would return to normal.

I applied for a part-time job at the noncommissioned officers' club. The position I applied for was a cook position working the evening shift from seven to ten. I went to the interview and was hired and worked several evenings per week. I used the money that I earned from the club to live on there.

When Beulah and the kids were ready to come to Germany, she contacted me, and I instructed her on the procedures to follow. She contacted the transportation office and gave them copies of my orders reassigning me to Germany. She made arrangements for the furniture and other household items to be packed and shipped to Germany. She also picked up the plane tickets for the family and shipped the vehicle to Germany. She had previously applied for and received the passports. The family had to fly to New York to get a flight to Germany.

Beulah and the kids had to go to McGuire Air Force Base in New Jersey and check into billeting because the flight did not depart until the following day. Our two granddaughters were traveling with the family, and my wife had to carry them to the airport prior to her flight departure, because they could not fly with her. Once they were on their flight, my wife and the kids returned to McGuire Air Force Base and waited until the next day to return to New York for their departure.

When Beulah and the kids arrived at the airport she informed me that our granddaughters arrived in Frankfurt, Germany, on a different flight. My friend and I met them at the airport and collected their luggage. We were approximately one hour's drive from the base.

When we arrived at the base, the house was ready to occupy. I had gone to the commissary during the week prior to the families arrival and purchased food for the family. I had also picked up some sheets, blankets, pillows, and some other household items. When our household items arrived, I returned the items to the housing office. Everyone was exhausted from the long flight.

The following day, I contacted an individual about picking up my vehicle and transporting it to Spangdahlem Air Base. The vehicle was delivered within one week, and the family visited several places off base on the economy. We enjoyed the country during the winter months when the snow was on the trees and in the country areas. The buildings were painted with different colors, and the snow made them seem like they were on a postcard. The kids enjoyed Germany, and they were enrolled in school and made new friends. I was informed that I had to pay for our granddaughters to attend school. I contacted the legal office on base and was informed to complete paperwork that would prevent me from paying for my grand-daughters to attend school.

> The Federal Republic of Germany is located in the heart of Europe. Germany is in the center of nine neighboring states. Denmark in the north, Netherlands, Belgium, Luxemburg and France in the west. Switzerland and Austria in the south, and the Czech Republic and Poland in the east. The country boasts a great cultural diversity, charming towns and attractive landscapes. Spangdahlem Air Base is located in the Federal State of Rheinland-Pfalz. About 20 miles Northeast of the city of Trier in the southwest section of Germany along the borders of Belgium, Luxembourg and France. The Bitburg Annex, which adds to the base space and facilities, is located about 10 miles from Spangdahlem in the city of Bitburg. This region is known as the Eifel. Internet en.wiki.bedia/. org/9wiki/Spagdahlem_Air Base.

There was a squadron of wild weasel aircraft and F-15 also at Spangdahlem Air Base. After being in Germany for several months, Beulah informed me that she wanted to return to California to be near the older kids if they required assistance. I made the arrangements with the transportation office to have the furniture packed and shipped to the United States. I picked up the airplane tickets for the family to fly home. I drove them to the airport, and we said our goodbyes, and they departed for the States. I returned to

Spangdahlem Air Base and had applied for a room in the barracks prior to the family's departure. I hired a cleaning person to clean the house that we had occupied and returned the keys to the housing office. I also contacted an individual on base to drive my vehicle to the port and ship it to the States. I really wanted my family to remain in Germany with me. I did not want to be separated from them. I wanted the kids to have both of us present and not just one parent. I had left them in California when I came to Germany. I decided that I was tired of this type foolishness and would not permit it to occur again. I decided when I received another assignment, we all would go together.

When the family returned to California, Beulah located a house for them, and they settled into their new home. I wrote to her and called on the phone as often as I could. She found a job and began working to earn some extra money. I sent my entire military pay check to her so she could take care of the family. One good point in her favor was that she could shop in the commissary and use the other base facilities. I was required to serve a thirty-six-month tour after my family returned to the United States. I realized that I would be in Germany for three years, and I had two choices to make. I could play sports for three years and end up with a sore body at the end of the tour. The second choice I had was to enroll in a university and receive a degree at the end of the tour. I decided to enroll in a business management curriculum. I attended class in the beginning during the lunch hour Mondays through Fridays. I also attended classes at night when I was not working at the club. I was so busy with homework from school that books were scattered all over my desk the entire semester.

I remember when I enrolled in an accounting course, a friend that worked with me was also in the class. The class was difficult for him and I, but his wife had taken the class a semester before we enrolled. We would meet once per week when we had problems to solve. His wife assisted us with the problems when we could not solve them. Both of us were successful in the course and received a passing grade. I was also required to complete a math course before I could graduate. I had been enrolled in other classes but did not take math classes. I decided that I had to complete the math class successfully, and I did just that. There were numerous management classes that I was required to complete. I completed all the classes successfully with passing grades. When I was not at work during the day or night, I was in my room studying and working on papers that were due. I maintained a list of courses that I was required to complete. When I completed a class, I crossed it off the list. I could now see the end of the tunnel in sight.

Everyone was going on vacation in Europe, but I did not have the opportunity or money to visit other countries. I was enrolled in classes at Troy State University for three years. I had to concentrate on my classes to ensure that I was successful. I enrolled in two classes per semester because the class load would guarantee that I would graduate before I left Germany. The difficulty of the classes was the deciding factors on how many classes that I would enroll in.

During the three years that I was enrolled in classes, I made plans to return to the States to visit my family in Fairfield, California. Normally in January of each year, I began to save money to purchase my plane ticket to fly to the States in December. I always went home in December to celebrate Christmas with my family. I would make my reservation in June or July for a flight in December. My flight departed from Frankfurt, Germany, for San Francisco, California. My wife always met me at the airport, and I normally remained with the family for thirty days. This gave me the opportunity to visit friends during my vacation at home. Also during my time at home, I visited my daughter's school to meet with her teachers. The teachers would give me an update on her progress in school. During this time, my wife and I had the opportunity to spend some time together. We would always attempt to do as many things together as possible, before I had to return to Germany. When it was time for me to leave, she drove me to the airport in San Francisco, California.

Sometimes there were military flights from the States to Germany. When I attempted to catch a flight, I had to sign up at the base that the flight was departing from. I was also required to be in military uniform and report to the terminal at the base. Sometimes I did not get on the first flight that was departing. When this occurred, I would be in the terminal for two to three days waiting for a flight with other military members. We also slept in the terminal because we did not have money to check into billeting or a hotel. When attempting to fly on a military flight, I would be required to fly from Dover Air Force Base in Dover Delaware or Charleston Air Force Base in South Carolina. When a military member was going permanent change of station or on emergency leave, they took priority over me and other military members returning from regular leave. During my career in the military, I did not always have additional money to spend for plane fare. Sleeping in the terminals was part of the experiences of being in the military that I had to endure along with many other military members.

On one of my days after I returned to Germany and reported to work, all my personal items were packed and placed into a box under the desk. My immediate supervisor informed me that his manager wanted me to come to work for him. I was comfortable working in the Plans Division and did not want to move to another section. I was informed by my supervisor that his manager wanted to meet with me to discuss the move. When we met, the colonel informed me that he wanted me to come work for him. I explained to the colonel that I was happy working for the lieutenant colonel. The person that worked in the position that worked for the colonel was responsible for assigning other military members to different details that occurred. The colonel asked me if I preferred to perform details or decide who performed the details. When I gave the colonel my answer, he knew that I would be working for him.

The colonel's assistant was completely different from him. The colonel was the director of operations and a very good manager to work for. He was a Mormon and did not drink coffee or smoke. There was an E7 master sergeant in charge of the section, and he became my immediate supervisor. I became the Unit Assistant Chief, Deputy Commander for Operations Administration. I was responsible for administrative management within the director of operations staff agencies. I reviewed all correspondence and action items and relieved the director of operation of those not requiring his attention.

When I arrived at work each day I picked up all message traffic for the director of operations. The message traffic had to be stamped and placed in a folder and be ready for the colonel to review when he arrived. I also informed him that there was message traffic for his review. The folder was placed on his desk, and after his review, he gave the folder back to me. I made the appropriate distribution of the messages to different agencies. The colonel also had a civilian secretary near his office that performed typing task and nonmilitary duties. The military task was performed by my supervisor and me. I ordered forms and publications for each subaccount that came under the operation office.

When classified material arrived in the office, I was responsible for signing for the material. After signing for the material, I had to ensure that the material was properly secured inside the safe. When publications became superseded, they had to be destroyed. There was paperwork for each classified document in the office safes. The publications that became obsolete had to be burned. There were some unclassified publications that I maintained in the office. Some of these publications had to be safeguarded due to the content. I exercised supervisory responsibility over six divisions and three tactical fighter squadrons.

During my time in Germany, numerous military members and their families were going on tours and vacations in Europe. I could not take advantage of the opportunities because 90 percent of my time was used for working, and the other 10 percent for school. I went on one tour during my time in Germany, and that was during a holiday while I was not in school.

After the family returned to the United States, I purchased a used vehicle and later moved into an apartment in the country. I lived on the third floor in the apartment building. My landlord and her family lived on the first floor. She was from France, and her husband was a retired Chief Master Sergeant. I lived in a two-bed room apartment with one bath and a kitchen. Sometimes during the months of November, I baked sweet potato pies and gave some of them to the landlord.

My friend Myron Webb had been stationed with me in Vietnam and at Homestead Air Force Base in Florida. When he arrived in Germany, he temporarily moved in with me until his daughter and son came to live with him. He moved into one of the apartments in the building that we lived in. I enjoyed living in the country being away from the base. I joined the Masonic Lodge and began to go through the required training to become a Master Mason. This was a new experience for me, and I was interested in learning as much as possible. We were issued booklets and other material to study. We also had scheduled meetings during the months. I went through three steps with other brothers and became a Master Mason.

I realized my time in Germany was coming to a close, and I had to prepare for the move. I received notification from the base personnel center that I had an assignment to Holloman Air Force Base in New Mexico. I decided to purchase a new Dodge Caravan and had it shipped to Reno, Nevada. I informed my wife that I had purchased a new vehicle, and she

FROM THE PAST TO THE PRESENT

could pick it up in Reno, Nevada. Three months prior to my departure from Germany, I completed the requirements for a Bachelor of Science degree in human resource management from Troy State University.

When I received my permanent change of station orders, I forwarded some copies to my wife so she could arrange to have the household goods packed and shipped to New Mexico. Finally the days were near for me to depart from Germany. I was ready to be moved to Technical Sergeant (E6) during my tour in Germany. Before leaving Germany, I sold my used vehicle to a young airman that worked for me. I processed out from the squadron and boarded my flight to California. My supervisor wrote the following comments on my performance:

> Staff Sergeant Hodge is truly an outstanding Non commissioned Officer. Professionalism, initiative and dedication are his hallmarks. As Assistant Chief, Deputy Commander for Operations (DO) Administration, he has demonstrated the ability to handle the myriad of extremely demanding administrative duties involved in managing six complex divisions for publications and forms with little or no supervision. His greatest asset is his leadership ability. Although Staff Sergeant Hodge does not have personnel under his supervision, many airmen seek him for advice and to discuss their personal problems. He is a very tactful Noncommissioned Officer who handles every individual and administrative problem with patience and diplomacy. During this reporting period, Staff Sergeant Hodge successfully completed several college courses while pursuing a degree in Human Resource Management. He received a Bachelor of Science degree with a minor in Social Science. Staff Sergeant Hodge realizes the value of a good education which helps in his military duties and prepares him for life in general. Staff Sergeant Hodge is a recognized expert in his field. His superior performance and drive has significantly contributed to the 52d Tactical Fight Wing's mission accomplishment. I highly recommend him for promotion ahead of his contemporaries, as

rarely have I seen a more dedicate self-disciplined and motivated Noncommissioned Officer.

When I arrived in California, my wife met me at the airport, and I was happy and excited to be home. She had gone to Reno, Nevada, to pick up the new dodge caravan, and she was driving the vehicle when she arrived at the airport. We returned home, and she had already contacted the transportation office and set up a packing and pick up date for the household goods.

Several days later the movers arrived at our residence and packed the household goods. The household goods were loaded on the truck, and the driver began the drive to New Mexico. We cleaned the house and returned the keys to the landlord. We enjoyed our drive to New Mexico because we had not driven through the States before.

When we arrived at Holloman Air Force base, I went to the housing office to check on the status of our house. I was informed by the housing personnel that it would be thirty days before we would receive a house on base. We decided to rent a trailer home because it was less expensive than a house or apartment. The trailer park was located approximately five miles from the base. The temperature was very hot during the day and cold at night. There were spiders and rattlesnakes in the area. We moved into the trailer and settled in for our new adventure in New Mexico.

The following day we registered Gloria in school, and we were informed that there was a corporal punishment policy at the school. The teachers spanked the children when they deemed it necessary with authorization. I informed the teachers that I could not give them authorization to spank my daughter. They informed me that whenever Gloria was in trouble, they would call me, and I had to respond. I worked about one mile from the school, and whenever a call came from the school, I went there without any hesitation.

Later during the day, I visited the squadron to process. The squadron was being established, and we were in a new building. Everything in the building and all the vehicles and equipment were also new. The mission of the squadron was classified, and everyone assigned to the squadron was required to have a security clearance prior to their assignment. There were only officers and Noncommissioned Officers (NCOs) assigned to the squadron who were military members that had been in the military for years with experience in different career fields.

When I processed into the squadron, I met my coworkers and supervisor. My supervisor was a lieutenant colonel, and he was dedicated and a hard worker. I was assigned as the noncommissioned officer in charge in logistics administration. I was responsible for administrative management of all chief of logistics staff agencies. I reviewed all correspondence and action items and relieved the lieutenant colonel of those not requiring his personal attention. I developed policies and interpreted directives necessary for effective administration. I exercised administrative responsibility over five sections. I processed all military documents for the logistics section. I ensured that appropriate control of classified documents were used when handling these documents. I reviewed, edited, and typed all section awards and decorations. I also was the self-inspection monitor and the logistics suggestion program manager.

We continued to get adjusted to the New Mexico area. We visited El Paso, Texas, and Las Cruz, New Mexico, on weekends. Both cities were larger than Alamogordo, New Mexico, and my wife and children could shop and purchase items not available there. On Friday nights when we were in Alamogordo, New Mexico, we went down town to purchase catfish and hush puppies. We checked out movie tapes from the library on base for the children. We used the base facilities as much as possible. The commissary was used to make food purchases, and the shopette was used to purchase some items. The pharmacy was used to purchase the family medication. We visited the hospital for doctor visits. I visited the dental office on base, and the family members had to go downtown for dental work. The commander of the squadron was a colonel (06). When the squadron was in the process of being established, there were luncheons set up by the squadron wives. The luncheons gave the squadron personnel a chance to become acquainted.

My wife began to work at the shopette on base in the afternoon. When she came home at night, she always brought potato chips and dip. I began to sit up my office and order forms to operate the office. Some of the other military in the squadron were also sitting up their office. The squadron did not have any lower-ranking airmen assigned to the squadron. The Noncommissioned Officers were (E-4s) and above. Each NCO was an expert in their career fields and had years of experience. The squadron required airmen with experience and they had to be able to function on their own without direct supervision. I continued to set up my office and order file cabinets and desk. New trucks began to arrive in the maintenance department. Each airmen in the Squadron lived on the base. The trucks were used to complete the squadron mission.

> The squadron is located on Holloman Air Force Base New Mexico near Alamogordo New Mexico. Holloman Air Force Base was originally established in 1942 as Alamogordo Air Field six miles west of Alamogordo New Mexico. It was renamed in 1948 after Colonel George Holloman, a Rich Square North Carolina native who was a pioneer in early rocket and pilot less air-craft research. The base Supports about 21,000 active duty, guard, reserve, retirees, DOD civilians and their family members. Personnel from Holloman have participated in numerous operations, such as Desert Shield/Desert Storm, Enduring Freedom, Iran Freedom and many more. Internet en.wiki.pedia.org/wiki/ Holloman_Air_ Base.

The weather during the summer months was very hot. It is not unusually to see tumbleweed blowing across the street on and off base. Airmen new to the base will become adjusted to the temperatures after approximately several weeks. We used the base theater to watch new movies that we did not check out from the base library. My coworkers and I got together on weekends and went fishing. Sometime we fished at night, and we would build a bonfire so we could see the tangurical spiders if they came in our direction. Sometimes one of the squadron members would give a barbecue at his home and invite the other members. Everyone in the squadron was new to the area and we met for the first time when we arrived at Holloman Air Force Base.

During the winter months, the temperatures were cold and required the wear of a coat. The wives of the squadron personnel scheduled a luncheon to give the wives a chance to meet and get acquainted. I concentrated on my duties of getting the requirements of my office met. Once everything began to function, I received a new airman in the office. He was a young airman from another base. Once he was processed, I started him on upgrade training and explained the squadron mission to him. He assisted me in the office with the office duties to ensure all requirements were met.

During the basketball season, I joined the squadron over thirty-five years old team. Each squadron member had a choice of what team they became a member of. Some older members could not run with the younger airmen. We played our games in the afternoon. My daughter accompanied me to the games because her mother would be at work. I enjoyed being on the court running and getting exercise.

Makita and Carmella, our granddaughters, came to live with us. We had to drive to Albuquerque, New Mexico, to pick them up. The drive was eight hours from Alamogordo, New Mexico. They attended the same school that Gloria was attending. I always attempted to go to the store without informing them where I was going. When they caught me, I had to reduce my purchases to purchase the snacks they wanted. There are spiders, scorpions, and rattlesnakes in New Mexico. We had to check the beds before going to sleep at night to ensure they were free of scorpions.

Each morning we checked our shoes for scorpions because they crawled into the shoes. We were at Holloman Air Force Base for one year, and I decided to cross train into another career field. Once the squadron was up and functional, several airmen began to search for assignments to other bases. I applied for retraining into the boom operator's career field.

Several weeks after applying for retraining, I was contacted and informed by the personnel office that the career field was not short of personnel. I had to select a different career to cross train into. I selected the Club Management career field to cross train into. I did not attend school but was informed that I would train on the job. I was assigned to Grand Forks Air Force base in North Dakota.

When I received my permanent change of station orders, the transportation office was contacted to schedule the packing and pick up of the household goods. Once the furniture was packed and loaded on the truck, we moved into the billeting quarters on base. We removed the nails from the walls and filled the nail holes. The shower walls were washed and cleaned. The water spots were removed by using glass cleaner. Oil spots in the driveway were removed by pouring cat litter on the spots and removing it. The inspectors came from the housing office and inspected the house and

I returned the keys. The drive to California was a good trip and we took pictures of some areas while driving along the freeway.

When we arrived in Fairfield, California, the search for a home began. We located a house, and I contacted the transportation office to schedule a delivery date for the furniture. When the furniture arrived, the delivery personnel unloaded the furniture. My wife instructed them where to place each item. I checked each item off on the inventory sheets. Once everything was unloaded, we checked each item for damage. We had to file a claim with the legal office for each item that was damaged or lost. I remained in California for several weeks and then flew to Grand Forks Air Force Base in North Dakota. My boss wrote the following performance comments.

> Technical Sergeant Hodge is a truly superior non commissioned officer. Having arrived at a time when only part time clerical support was available for the Logistics Branch, he faced the formidable task of establishing an entire administration section from the ground up in support of a logistics function unlike any other in the Air Force. Technical Sergeant Hodge met the challenge and demonstrated why he was the perfect choice for a position that was sole administrative support for forty-three people. On his own, through self-tutoring, He qualified himself on the squadron word processing equipment, thus saving the squadron $700.00 in TDY and training expense. As the logistics branch faced a shortage of assigned personnel TSgt Hodge volunteered for additional duties as host tenant agreement monitor, unit training representative, unit resource manager, plans and programs monitor, and self inspection monitor. A workload few office personnel see in their entire career and little background in any of these areas. Technical Sergeant Hodge accomplished each additional duty with the aplomb of an experienced professional. Technical Sergeant Hodge's motivation, initiative, and dedication to excellence set him apart from his peers.

I arrived at Grand Forks Air Force Base in November, and the temperature was thirty below zero, and there was four feet of snow on the ground. I was not prepared for the cold weather because I had never been in this type of weather before. I was assigned to the 321st Combat Support Group. I was unaccompanied and was assigned a room in the barracks. I arrived at the base on the weekend. On Monday I was issued cold weather gear and turned in records to the personnel office. I processed into the squadron after completing the processing at the base personnel office. The personnel office was located approximately one mile from the barracks. I did not have a vehicle at the base so I had to walk to the personnel office. When the inprocessing procedures was completed, I walked to the officers' club where I was assigned. I was introduced to my supervisor who was a retired military member. He was also a civil servant and was rated as a GS-11. My supervisor escorted me through the club to each area and introduced me to the employees. I was also introduced to the morale and welfare staff and the commander.

The clubs throughout the air force had previously received appropriate support from the government. The support had been discontinued and the clubs had to be self-sufficient. The club managers had to develop more programs to generate more sales. The labor cost is one of the highest cost on the club financial statement. This cost affected the bottom line and was the deciding factor in making a profit or having a loss. I was placed on upgrade training and put in charge of the employees and bars. My supervisor informed me that if I was in charge of a department I had to know how it worked. I began to learn all the things about the bar operations by setting up the bar, stocking it, and cutting the fruit.

I performed the inventory of each item in the bar. I picked up the supplies to restock the bar when a brand became low. I picked up the bar supplies from the class 6 store on base. I was trained on how to perform inventories of the entire club. I studied the club regulations and policies. I worked in the kitchen assisting the chef on food preparation. I assisted in the setup of food preparations for parties and special functions. I trained on how to read a financial statement and determine what needed to be changed in the club. I was also trained on how to calculate the food cost of each menu item. My duty title at the club was assistant club manager.

> Grand Forks Air Force Base is a United States Air Force base located north of Emerado, North Dakota and is approximately 16 miles west of Grand Forks North Dakota. In the 2010 census, the base was counted as a CDP with a total population of 2,367. www.grandforks. af.mil.http//civil-rights.findlaw.cotherconstitutional-rig.

During my assignment at the club I developed organizational structure and planned workloads for open mess functions. I requisitioned and ordered supplies and equipment from authorized sources. I provided controls for equipment, space, and materials. I established work methods and performance standards for functions associated with open mess operations. I also recommended food, beverages, and entertainment requirements.

After being there for several months, Beulah called and informed me that the family would be joining me in North Dakota. I made the arrangements with the housing office to obtain a house on base. I was scheduled to attend the Club Management School in Biloxi, Mississippi. I informed Beulah that I would be away at school for eight weeks when they arrived at Grand Forks Air Force Base. I had become good friends with the class 6 store manager. I informed him to give my wife and family any assistance she required once they arrived on base.

I had stated when I was in Biloxi, Mississippi, in 1969, I did not want to go there again because of the treatment of my people. The year was 1986, and I was going there again to attend club school for eight weeks. I went to the base personnel office, and my temporary duty orders were printed. The next stop I made was at the accounting and finance office. I requested advance payments for my time that I would be in Mississippi. I used the money to live on and purchase food items why there. I also had to visit the transportation office to pick up plane tickets for my trip to Mississippi and a return trip to Grand Forks, North Dakota.

Once I completed everything required for my trip, I contacted my friend and informed him that I wanted him to give me a ride to the airport. When I arrived in Biloxi, Mississippi, I noticed that some things had been changed for the good of the people. I was considered to be permanent party, and I did not have a curfew. Some of the students that were not permanent party at the school had a curfew, and they had to be in the barracks by a certain time. I arrived on base during the weekend, and this gave me a chance to become familiar with the base. I was required to be in class and on time beginning Monday morning along with my classmates. We were required to be in the proper uniform and ready for inspection before class began. I was assigned to a room in the barracks during the time I was in school. There was a dining room in the barracks that I visited sometimes.

I purchased food from the commissary to place in my refrigerator such as, bologna, bread, peanut butter, crackers, jelly, hot dogs, potato chips, TV dinners, and potted meat. These were food items that I lived on when I was unable to attend the dining hall. This also prevented me from spending money each day that I could not afford to spend. Classes began each morning at 7:00 a.m. and ended at 5:00 p.m. We were given one hour for lunch and three fifteen-minute breaks each day during classes. Sometimes I visited the Noncommissioned Officers' club on Fridays for lunch. I did not return to the barracks because the location was too far away for me to make it back to class on time.

During class we were instructed how to read a financial statement. I also learned about labor cost, food cost, safeguarding funds, and everything pertaining to club operations. We were given a test every Friday that covered all material that we had reviewed and discussed during the week. Each class member was required to score 70 percent on the test. My classmates and I got together at night after class to study for each test that was given.

I awoke on a Saturday morning and decided to visit Biloxi, Mississippi, to search for a barbershop where I received haircuts in 1969. I decided to walk to search for the shop. When I located the shop, the owner was there, and when he saw me, he remembered that I visited his shop in 1969. There was a sign that listed pictures of different hair styles that the barbers cut for the customers. The same sign in the shop was there in 1969 the last time I was in the shop. The owner and I discussed issues that occurred during the time that I was there before. I explained to him that I was only there temporarily and would return to North Dakota after I completed the class.

On weekends we could go anywhere we desired, but we had to ensure that we were in class on Monday morning. On a particular weekend, a classmate that lived in Florida decided to drive home for the weekend. I decided to ride with my classmate to Florida because Myron Webb, my friend, lived there. I planned to visit him and his family when we arrived in Florida. We had been stationed together at several bases earlier in our military careers. The weekend was the first and only one that I left the state prior to completing school. Normally on weekends I would visit the movies and Base Exchange. I did not have a lot of money to spend, and I had to limit my activities. I also was in my room for a great amount of time on weekends because of limited funds.

I remember one weekend a civilian worker from the base had a barbecue at his home and invited the class to come over. Some of my classmates attended the barbecue and had a great time. The pig was placed in the ground on hot coals and cooked until it was completely done. This was my first experience eating chopped barbecue, and it was delicious. I informed some of the classmates that they missed a treat.

The Noncommissioned Officers' club had some activity going on and I stopped there on Friday or Saturday nights for several hours. On Sundays I prepared for the upcoming week, which consisted of class studies and ensuring that my uniforms were clean. There was a classmate whose name is Gus. Gus was from Texas, and we got together to study before the test was given on Fridays. Each week I looked forward to completing the course, because I wanted to be home with my family. Some of my classmates went out to restaurants and clubs every night. I did not have the money to accompany them, and I stayed in my room most of the time. I remember a classmate that was out all night during class weekdays, and sometimes he arrived minutes before the class began.

Finally the day arrived, and we were given the final examination. The entire class passed the test, and everyone was ready to return home. Some classmates exchanged phone numbers and promised to keep in touch. Several of the classmates called after returning home to their states; they were starting new programs. When a classmate had a program at their club that was generating sales, they passed the information on to others to try at their club. I had obtained several new ideas and procedures from the school that I instituted at my club. I used different programs at the club to bring customers in for the variety of foods and entertainment. There were young officers at the club, so I started a disco program for them. I started a kiddies night for the children because the parents would be forced to bring them to the club, and they would participate. Each program was designed to attract the club member and their family. The clubs throughout the military had become more family oriented.

Keesler Air Force Base is located in Biloxi Mississippi. This is the training center for airmen who have just completed basic training as well as additional training they will need for future assignments. Students receive instructions in the field of electronics, such as cryptography, ground radio, wideband maintenance and office administration. The base houses the medical group which is the second largest Air Force medical center. Keesler Air Force Base is one of the principal technical training wings in the USAF, and in Air Education and Training Command (AETC). (Enipedia.org/wiki/ Keesler_AFB.)

Gloria, our daughter, was attending school off base in Grand Forks, North Dakota, and Clifford was working part-time at the Base Exchange. Gloria was in different after school programs, and she was required to attend practices after school. On numerous occasions I had to drive through snow and ice to transport her to school as well as pick her up from school. I remember a play she was in called *The Little Shop of Horror*. When the play was presented at her school, the auditorium was full with parents and students. My wife still maintains the brochure that was published listing *The Little Shop of Horror* program and each participant's name.

The schools were very seldom closed due to bad weather, and I had to ensure that I was available to pick her up after school when she stayed over. She enjoyed attending school and did not want to miss a day from school, unless she was ill. I remember on one occasion my friend who is a deer hunter and I went to pick her up in his van. He had placed some deers in his vehicle weeks prior. She was riding in the back part of the van and informed me later that she would not ride there again.

I began to work on different programs at the club to increase sales at the club. My supervisor and I started a food-delivery program on base only. We previously visited several restaurants to determine what food items were purchased during the lunch period. We discovered that salads were a hot seller to women during the lunch period. We instructed the chef to calculate the cost of a salad based on the ingredients and container size. After the cost was calculated, we selected a container that would be used for the salads. When the program was started, my supervisor and I visited different offices and asked the employees if they wanted to purchase a salad. We placed the containers on a sheet pan with ice around the salads to maintain the proper temperature.

When the delivery program began, we set up a phone in the kitchen area where salad orders were placed. The delivery program generated additional sales for the dining section. When the program was well on the way, I discussed the idea with my supervisor about delivering hot foods to the employees during the winter months. He informed me that he did not think the idea would work. I informed him to give me a chance to experiment with the idea before giving up on the idea. I made a list of foods that patrons could purchase during cold weather. I gave the food list to the chef, and she developed a food cost for each item.

The next step involved determining how the food would be kept hot until it was delivered to the customers. I purchased a food carrier and placed two sterno cans into the carrier. When I checked the temperature of the food, it cooked because the temperature was too hot. I removed one steno can, and the food temperature was good. During the rainy and cold snow days, the delivery business was great. We had to hire a delivery driver to deliver the food items. We were the first in the military to start a delivery service at Grand Forks Air Force Base. The delivery service worked well and increased the food sales.

The air force inspectors were impressed with the delivery service. We offered tacos on Tuesday nights and called it Taco Tuesday. I ensured that the dining ins, dining outs, farewells, and special functions were placed on the priority list for service. These functions were very important, and high-ranking civilians, noncommissioned officers, and their spouses were in attendance.

The largest and most important function ever held at the Grand Forks Air Force Officers Club was the B1-B Reception. This was a reception that was given to welcome the first B1-B aircraft to the base. The supervisor and I worked with different committees to plan the events and the menu. One committee selected the type of foods to be served at the reception. There was a committee that decided the type of table setup and arrangements. The commanders informed my manager and I to order new silverware, glasses, table cloths, table skirtings, and anything required to make the reception a success. Some parts of the club had to be remodeled before the day of the reception. The carpet throughout the entire club was replaced with new carpet.

Finally the day of the reception arrived, and the club staff was ready. The ballroom was set, and the tables were skirted. The new pans and silverware was place on the tables. Blocks of ice were carved into different figures and advertised in certain locations. The different food items were placed on the tables in appropriate locations. The dignitaries, senators, and congressmen began to arrive at the club. Everyone entered the ballroom, which was decorated beautifully with displays throughout the room. There were also special guests speakers at the reception. The club staff ensured that the reception was a success, and we did not receive any complaints.

The next year I was selected to attend culinary school for two weeks at Lackland Air Force Base in Texas. The instructors taught the students how to set up tables for different functions. I learned how to prepare different meals and read receipts. I learned how to prepare sauces for different meals. We were taught the wines to select to serve with different meals. We were trained on the different types of convection ovens used to cook foods. The class was divided into two groups. One team worked in the kitchen with the chefs and was taught how to prepare the meals. The second team was taught how to arrange the tables and what tables to use. They were also taught how to set up the dining room. The class was given the final project that involved preparing a meal for the class, and everyone sat down for dinner. After dinner the team responsible for cleanup entered the kitchen area and returned the area to the original setup.

I completed the class and returned to Grand Forks Air Force Base and continued my duty as assistant club manager. I also enrolled in a computer class to become more proficient in my career field. I had been informed prior to my arrival at Grand Air Force Base that I would be there for one year. Now it was almost three years since I arrived at Grand Forks Air Force Base, and I did not have an assignment.

I remember the first time I was driving in a snowstorm. The snow froze on the wiper blades when I was driving from the city of Grand Forks to the base. Every military member was required to maintain a survival kit in their vehicle. The survival kits contained items that would enable everyone inside a vehicle to survive if the vehicle stopped in a snowstorm. During the winter months when the temperatures were below freezing, most military members limited their travel to the base and local area. Some military members and their families were afraid to adventure outside the base, and they developed cabin fever. During the winter months the only animals visible were snow rabbits. The vehicles were placed inside garages, and an electrical cord was connected to a cord connected to the vehicle engine. This procedure prevented the oil in the engine from freezing.

I had purchased a Toyota vehicle for $200, and it was rusty, and there was a hole in the floor. I parked the vehicle outside the garage, and when I went outside each morning, it started all the time. I parked my Dodge Caravan in the garage each night, and sometimes it would not start up due to the cold weather. When this happened, my friend came to our residence and we attempted to jump start the vehicle. Sometimes we could start the vehicle, but most of the time I had to leave it in the garage. We did not let the cold weather prevent us from coming out and going to the doctor and commissary on base. We limited our travel to the city of Grand Forks to picking our daughter up from school.

I knew all the commanders and their spouses because they attended functions at the club. The spouses had a wives club that met at the club to plan functions. My manager informed me to always remember to give the commanders' wives anything they requested. He stated that the wives controlled the commanders, and they controlled the money. When we were required to purchase items for the club, the commanders donated funds for the purchases. The club was required to make a profit each month. There were meetings setup with the commanders each month to review the financial status of the club. When the club financial statement was reviewed by the commanders and club manager, an explanation was required when there was money lost. The commanders required that steps be presented to prevent a lost for the next month. Different programs were continuously being used to bring members into the club to generate sales.

I remember one program that we instituted was a Hawaiian luau. This was done during the winter, and the weather was very cold, and there was snow on the ground. I contacted the civil engineering team, and they delivered a dump truck of sand to the club. The sand was dumped inside the ballroom. The club staff placed a volleyball net in the sand and decorations were placed throughout the ballroom. The tables were placed on the floor, and all participants wore Hawaiian clothing. Hawaiian food was served, and Hawaiian music was played during the night. The club members and their guests sat on the floor and ate their food.

On Mother's Day, Thanksgiving, and Easter, a buffet line was set up, and the members served themselves. The club made a numerous amount of money on these holidays. Once per month the club offered all-you-can-eat crab night, and the support was great. These are some of the food programs we offered to generate sales for the dining room.

The club member's club dues were increased to generate income for the club. The club council and the commanders had to approve the dues' increase before it could be implemented. I continued to implement different programs to increase the club sales. I enjoyed the tour in North Dakota, but I did not care for the cold winter days. Our home did not become hot during the winter due to the cold temperatures. The vehicle heaters did not become hot because the weather was so cold.

When I was not working at the club during the warm weather, my wife and I went fishing in the Red River. I remember on one occasion we were fishing at night and my wife was sleeping in the car. My hook was hit by a fish, and I held the rod in one hand and the net in the other hand. I was screaming for her to come down to the river to assist me. She did not hear me calling her, so I managed to net the fish after bringing it to the bank.

Three years had passed, and I did not have an assignment to another base. My family and I were ready for a change of climate. I received a phone call that my father had become ill, and I realized that I should be near him. He had been suffering from heart problems. I contacted the base personnel office and inquired about being reassigned to Langley Air Force Base in Hampton, Virginia. The base is located three to four hours' drive from Martinsville, Virginia, where my father lived. I was informed by the assignment personnel that there were no openings in my career field at Langley Air Force Base. I was informed by the assignment personnel that the only way I could be assigned to Langley Air Force Base was to take an assignment to Osan Air Base in Korea and apply for a follow-on assignment to Langley Air Force Base.

I applied for the follow-on assignment to Langley Air Force Base, and it was approved. When certain personnel discovered that I was black, an attempt was made to cancel my assignment to Korea. I informed Beulah about the assignment and prepared the family for the move to Hampton, Virginia.

Once I received my permanent change-of-station orders, I contacted the transportation office and made arrangements to have the household goods packed and shipped to Hampton, Virginia. We decided to hire a house cleaner to clean the house. We moved into the temporary quarters until the house was cleaned. I processed out from the squadron and returned the keys to the housing office after the house was inspected. We left the base and began our drive to Hampton, Virginia.

We enjoyed the drive and scenery during the trip. When we arrived in Hampton, Virginia, we located a house for the family. The household goods arrived, and they were unpacked and placed in the house. I remained in Virginia with my family for thirty days and then departed for Osan Air Base in Korea. My supervisor wrote the following information concerning my performance:

> Technical Sergeant Hodge is a dedicated and highly competent professional who always exhibits Outstanding performance of assigned duties. He developed and implemented labor cost controls which ensured successful operations. He initiated numerous programs and daily Specials. The daily salad delivery service was the only delivery service of that type in the Air Force. He was responsible for the success of the B-1B reception held at the club. The Reception had numerous Very Important Persons (VIPs) and dignitaries in attendance. He was responsible for the completion of three offices and dining room renovations prior to the Reception. Technical Sergeant Hodge received many favorable comments for outstanding success of military protocol

functions he supervised. TSgt Hodge is highly motivated and produces Exceptional results. TSgt Hodge is a creative manager whose positive attitude enabled him to gain immeasurable productivity from his subordinates. TSgt Hodge should be assigned as the manager of a small open mess so he can increase his management skills and should be allowed to attend career related seminars, that further His career knowledge and expertise. TSgt Hodge is a high achiever who continually strives for improvement. Promote ahead of his peers.

My daughter and wife drove me to the airport, and I boarded the plane for Kimpo International airport in Seoul Korea. When I arrived, my sponsor was there to meet me. He was the manager of the Afterburner Club at Osan Air Base. When we arrived at Osan Air Base, I met my supervisor at the Challenger Club where I was assigned. He welcomed me to the squadron, and we discussed club issues, and then I departed for my apartment.

The afterburner club manager, and I shared a two-bedroom apartment together. He was from Texas and is a country and Western fan. I became familiar with the area during the weekend and visited the Challenger Club and met some of the employees.

On Monday morning I was processing into the squadron when the Morale Wellness and Recreation (MWR)commander came over and requested that I accompany him. He informed me that the Red Cross had sent a message and that my father had requested that I come home due to the death of my brother. I applied for emergency leave to return home, and it was approved. I caught a flight to the United States, and when I arrived in Martinsville, Virginia, my father had made all funeral arrangements.

My brother Robert Hodge was buried within a few days in the family cemetery. My father informed me that Robert had complained of having a headache before going to the hospital. He stated that the doctors informed him that my brother had died of natural causes. I remained with my father for a few days before going to California to spend a few days with my family. Several days were spent with my family, and then I caught a flight to Kimpo International Airport.

When I arrived, at Kimpo military transportation was available to Osan Air Base. The following day I went to the club and reviewed the financial statement and other papers. I began to order supplies and equipment from authorized sources. I developed organizational structure and planned workloads for open mess functions. I provided for and controlled the use of equipment, space, and materials. Work methods and performance standards for functions associated with open mess operations were established. I evaluated variances from approved budgets and monitored subsidiary financial transactions.

The club had been losing money for some time, and I began to put some procedures in place to stop the losses. One example was the table placemats that were being used and discarded after being used one time. The cost to the club was $3,000 per month. I had the lunch menu placed on one side of the mats, and the breakfast menu placed on one side. The mats were placed inside plastic covers and continued to be used over and over. The $3,000 charge to the club was eliminated.

Another procedure I implemented was to hire part-time waitress to serve special functions during the evening hours. This procedure eliminated overtime and prevented the day employees from working past eight hours. New food programs were started to increase food sales. The club members' dues were increased to generate income for the club. The club council had to approve the increase before placing the procedure into effect. The club sold keg beer that was shipped from the States. During the lunch period a special food item was placed in a plate and put in a display case. Each member that entered the club could review the special before entering.

When I decided to begin a new program, the Korean supervisors were informed, and their decisions were very important. I wrote my ideas on paper and gave the information to my secretary. She translated the information into the Korean language because some of the supervisors did not read and understand English. I received a second Red Cross message that another brother had passed away. My father had requested that I come home to be with the family during the time of their grievance. I caught a military flight from Osan Air Base Korea to North Carolina.

When I arrived in North Carolina, I caught a Greyhound bus from North Carolina to Martinsville, Virginia. When I arrived at home, my father informed me that the doctors informed him that my brother had died of natural causes. I could not believe that two of my brothers had passed away within two months. I remained with my father until the funeral was over.

One week later, I went to Hampton, Virginia, to visit my wife and daughter. My wife prepared Thanksgiving dinner because I would not be home for Thanksgiving. My wife and daughter drove me to the Washington National Airport area a day prior to my scheduled flight. This saved my wife and daughter from driving to the airport early in the morning and being in heavy traffic. I checked into a hotel overnight and departed for Korea on Thanksgiving Day. I called my wife from the hotel before I departed.

When I arrived back in Korea, I resumed my club duties. I had to become adjusted to the Korean culture to make life easier for the employees. The Korean employees accepted my ideas and suggestions. They realized that I was attempting new procedures that had never been done before. The new procedures and ideas increased the food sales and established job stability for the employees. The employees did not hesitate to give me advice on different ideas that I wanted to put in place.

I continued to introduce new food items and work on procedures to reduce labor. The club was scheduled for a partial renovation project. The club was also nominated for the Curtis E. Lemay Award. The award was one of the highest awards that a military club could receive. I began to review club paperwork to ensure that it was current. I informed the chef to review all receipt cards and ensure that each card was updated. The financial paperwork was reviewed by my boss and I. I ensured that club paperwork was in compliance with morale and welfare regulations policies.

When I had been working at the club for six months, a bottom line profit was made. This was the first time the club had shown a bottom line profit in years. The wing commander contacted my supervisor and requested to see my qualification to be a club manager. There were several other airmen in the club career field, but I was the only black manager. This was a slap in the face to me because I was more qualified than anyone on the base. I gave my supervisor my qualification, that is, completed leadership school, completed the NCO Academy, have an associate of arts degree, and a bachelor of science degree. I was also enrolled in a master of science degree program at that time. I also had completed culinary school and Open Mess Management school. I also had received four Air Force Commendation Medals and one Meritorious Service Medal. I felt that this was unfair and discrimination against me. He did not ask for the qualifications of the other airmen in club positions at the base. My supervisor submitted the information to the colonel that had requested it. Whenever the colonel attended a function at the club, he would contact me and ask if I needed anything. I knew he was requesting the information because I was black.

The Korean employees eventually went on strike, and all the American facilities such as the Base Exchange, shopette, commissary, and clubs were closed. The other club managers and I opened the officers' club and served breakfast, lunch and dinner to the club members. We prepared each meal for the members. I was happy to be working in the kitchen preparing food.

I remember on one occasion preparing several large pans of cream beef for breakfast. Some of the club members ate the cream beef for the first time at the club. My supervisor quit his job and went on leave for thirty days. I became the club manager when he stated that he quit.

All delivery trucks that arrived at the gate to enter the base were stopped and searched by the strikers. When the strike was over, business returned to, normal and the employees returned to work at the club. The Korean club manager was getting close to retirement, and the policy was that he select a replacement before he retired. The person he selected was not a good manager, and the club employees did not want to work for him. I selected a different person from within the club to be the club manager. After the selection, I scheduled a meeting with the employees to introduce the new manager. The employees accepted the new manager without any hesitation.

During my tour in Korea, I met numerous business people that owned stores in the city of Osan. Some of them visited the club for lunch and dinner. I ensured that they knew me and about my goals for the club and employees. I continued to stay busy creating new programs to increase sales and to make the club profitable. I joined the Masonic Lodge at Osan, Korea, and became active in the lodge. We assisted the children's orphanage home. During the year we paid for heating fuel for the home. We also painted the home, and during the summer months we scheduled cookouts for the children. The children were fathered by American service members, and the people did not support the home. I remained active in the lodge and continued to perform duties in the lodge. Later I joined the consistory and became a 32 degree in the lodge. The next step for me was to become a 33 degree Mason. I continued to perform my military duties and remained active in the lodge. I remained active in the lodge until I departed from Korea.

The Korean people lived in apartments, and there were buildings everywhere. Some business owners worked on the first floor and lived on the second floor in the apartment buildings. I remember after my arrival in Korea I went to a clothing store and gave the owner a picture from a magazine of an item I wanted him to make. The owner measured me to get my pants, shirt, and coat size. The measurement had to be taken only one time. Each time a new item was requested, the store owners referred to the original measurements that was originally taken.

When I decided to purchase shoes, I entered a store, and the owner instructed me to place my feet on a sheet of paper. The owner drew a diagram of my feet, and he measured across the top to get the width. From that moment on when I wanted to purchase shoes, I just had to inform him about the type of shoe and give him a picture. He did not need to take another measurement.

Numerous airmen have relocated back to the States and continue to order merchandise from the vendors in Korea. Name brand sneakers, purses, jackets, and other items were available for purchase, and they were inexpensive compared to the United States prices. I purchased some blankets and other items to send home to my wife. I continued to work in the club preparing it for the Curtis E. Le May award nomination. The club was going through a renovation. When the renovation was completed, the paperwork was submitted. After the selection process, the club did not get selected. The entire MWR staff was happy and excited that the club had been nominated. The nomination was the first for the club, and there should be many more.

I continued to work on programs to increase sales, and continued to take college classes at night. South Korea, officially known as the Republic of Korea (ROK; Korea is an East Asian country occupying the southern half of the Korean peninsula. To the North, it is bordered by north Korea (Democratic People's Republic of Korea) with which it was united until 1945. To the west, across the yellow sea, lies China and to the southeast, across the Korean strait lies Japan. The South Korean government's structure is determined by the constitution of the Republic of Korea. (Indicate source here.)

I realized that my job in Korea was complete and the tour had been served well. I had made some great accomplishments at the Challenger Club as the assistant club manager. When I received my permanent change-of-station orders, I scheduled a pickup of my hold baggage. I processed out from the squadron on Friday and informed my coworkers and employees that I would be leaving Korea on Sunday. The employees scheduled a going-away party for me at the club. I informed them that I had enjoyed my tour there, and they should be proud to be members of a great staff.

On Sunday morning I stopped at the club and ate breakfast and said my goodbyes to everyone. My coworker drove me to the Kimpo International airport, and I boarded the plane for Hampton, Virginia. The flight was a long flight, and I watched movies and slept to pass the time.

When I finally arrived in Hampton, Virginia, my wife and daughter were at the airport to meet me. I went on leave for thirty days before reporting to my new base of assignment. I reviewed my personnel records and the performance report written by my supervisor in Korea. I had started programs that had never been done before when I was in Korea. The employees were given new uniforms during my tour there. My primary goal was to make the club profitable and I accomplished that goal. I left Korea with my head held high because I knew that I had given my best. The employees gave me their full support because they realized that everything that I attempted was in their best interest. I contacted my father during my leave to check on his condition. When my leave ended, I reported to the squadron and processed into the unit. My performance report written by my previous supervisor reads as follows:

> Technical Sergeant Hodge is a dedicated professional who always exhibits outstanding performance of assigned duties. He initiated a multitude of revenue generating programs and Daily specials. He is responsible for the success of the monthly PME graduation ceremonies. The receptions had numerous VIP's and dignitaries in attendance. He was responsible for the reconstruction of a new menu, saving the club sizeable Expenditures.

TSgt Hodge received many favorable comments for the outstanding success of military protocol functions he has supervised. TSgt Hodge is highly Motivated and produces exceptional results. TSgt Hodge is a creative manager whose cooperation and positive attitude enable him to gain productivity from his subordinates. TSgt Hodge realized the importance of an education. He completed nine hours toward a Master of Science degree in Human Resource Management Systems. TSgt Hodge is a high achiever who continually strives for improvement. Promote.

When I arrived at the club, the manager and assistant manager did not know that I was scheduled to arrive. The club manager was a Senior Master Sergeant (SMSGT), and the assistant club manager was a Master Sergeant (MSGT). The installation club manager was assigned to the officers' club. He was a GM-14, and his assistant was a GS-9. My new supervisor was elated to have me at the club. After he introduced me to the staff, he drove me to the officers' club to meet the installation club manager. He informed me that he wanted me to work at the officers' club. I informed him that I would feel more comfortable working at the Noncommissioned Officers' club (NCO). He informed me that I could work at the NCO club with the understanding if my assistance was required at the officers' club, he would remove me from the NCO club.

The NCO club was a four-thousand member club, and the club had to become self-sufficient. In the past, some military clubs had been receiving appropriate support, but that support was going away. Each club throughout the military was required to generate the required amount of sales to pay for club operating expenses. We used the club directories and brochures to get new ideas to generate sales and bring new members into the club.

The first large revenue-generating program we instituted was a bingo program. We hired a bingo program manager to call the games and to manage the program. My boss and I also managed and called the games when the bingo manager was not available. The bingo program generated sales for the club and was successful.

During bingo nights at the club, which was on Monday nights, the games were held in the ballroom. The program generated sales for the dining room because the participants purchased food during the games. The program also generated sales for the bar because drinks were purchased from the bar. We also offered bar bingo games on Friday nights.

The next large revenue-generating program we started was bringing popular entertainers to the club to perform. Once we decided on what group or person we wanted to perform, we contacted their agency and inquired about the cost and availability. When everything was agreed upon with the club manager and the agency, a contract was developed. I developed a seating chart for the ballroom listing each table and seat location. I selected the appropriate number of seats we needed to sell to pay for the shows. This procedure prevented funds from being used from the club to pay for the events. The shows were enjoyed by the club members and their guests. During the nights that the entertainers were performing, sales for the dining room and other areas in the club increased.

The next large-generating program we started was an all-night disco, and patrons were charged at the door to enter the club. Funds were generated in the bar and dining room. On Friday nights we also offered an oyster bar for the patrons in the club. This was another food-generating event that we used to catch the customer when they walked pass the bar.

The next major generating program we decided to start was a delivery service on base. John, Fred, and I went to several pizza restaurants to review their operation. We gathered brochures and pamphlets from the restaurants and returned to the club and decided to offer pizza on the delivery service. We purchased a pizza press, frozen pizza balls, and premade pizza sauce. We made adjustments to the sauce to give it the taste we wanted. We also purchased all the condiments that was required for a pizza operation. We prepared receipt cards and calculated the food cost for each item that would be used to prepare and sell the pizza. The cooks began to prepare pizzas for club members to sample as part of the training program before the delivery service began.

The next adventure we performed was to visit restaurants that prepared steak subs. We observed employees at the restaurants preparing the steak subs. We purchased several steak subs and returned to the club and checked the subs to determine what items were placed on them. After we discovered how the subs were made, we had to decide the type of meat to use. We also performed a cost analysis to decide the cost we should charge for each sub.

We also decided to offer other food items such as hamburgers, french fries, fried chicken, hot wings, and hot dogs. The receipt cards were developed for all food items, and a menu was made listing each food item. The cooks began to prepare each menu item prior to the start of the delivery service. We did not know if the delivery service would be successful, so John, Fred, and I had to assist the delivery drivers.

On rainy and cold days, we had more orders than we could deliver. The delivery service continued to grow, and the sales were more than the dining room sales. We also delivered salads to customers that requested a light meal. My workday began at 7:30 a.m. on Mondays through Fridays and lasted until 9:30 p.m.

Each day that I arrived at work if there was a function scheduled in the ballroom at night, I had to assist the janitorial staff with the setup. When there were round tables there and the function required long tables, they had to be exchanged. When the ballroom was not set up and it was time for the delivery service to begin, I had to begin to deliver food. I continued to deliver food throughout the lunch period, which was at 11:00 a.m. to 1:00 p.m. After the delivery service was over, I normally had lunch with my supervisor, and we discussed club business. After completing lunch, I began to get the bingo material ready for the bingo manager. When there was a special function scheduled in the ballroom on Monday nights, the bingo program would be moved to another room or cancelled. On the nights that a special function was scheduled, I went to the kitchen and assisted with the plate preparation.

Fred was the food service manager over the kitchen. The food was placed on each plate and placed on wire racks that were placed in food warmers. When the food warmers were full, they were rolled to the nearest wall socket outside the ballroom and plugged in. They had to be placed out of view of the patrons. The silverware, glasses, salads, and salad dressing were placed on the tables prior to serving the food. Once the food was served, I assisted with removing the dishes from the tables and returning them to the kitchen.

During the weekdays business was normally slow. We met during the week to discuss ideas on how to increase the business. We catered wedding receptions during the week and weekends. We scheduled a disc jockey in one of the lounges to increase business. On Friday nights there was a disc jockey in each lounge except the casual lounge. There was a food special offered in the dining room each night. We offered an all-you-can-eat buffet with several food items during the lunch hours. We removed the long food pans and replaced them with short pans. The perception made the customers think there was more food on the buffet line. There were two meats and a salad on the buffet line. We also offered two vegetables and rolls on the buffet line.

On Fridays we offered fish for lunch, and the items were rotated each week. Sometimes we offered a roast beef on the bone with a carver to slice it. When each month ended, the other managers and I were required to perform an inventory of all items that was for sale in the club. Once the inventory was completed, the paperwork was forwarded to the Morale Welfare and Recreation Office (MWRO). The office personnel compared the paperwork with the sales and club expenditures for the month. This procedure determined if there was a profit or loss at the club. The labor cost was one of the most expensive cost in the club. Each manager concentrated on maintaining the labor cost at a level that would not affect the bottom line.

I continued to be involved in the management of the club operation. I had to remain physically fit because this was a military requirement. Each year I was required to run one and one-half mile within the required time. My military duty at the club was easy to perform because I was physically fit.

On Sundays a brunch buffet was offered at the club. I arrived at the club at 6:00 a.m. and unlocked the doors and issued the employees operating funds and food items. I also turned the cash registers on and ensured that they worked properly. We normally had a cashier and several cooks on duty for the Sunday brunch operations. Once the customers began to enter the club for brunch, I normally went out on the dock and fished until an employee called me for assistance. I also opened the casual bar on Sundays to serve the members and guests.

When the Sunday brunch was over, a snack line was set up in the casual bar area for the members. I normally remained at the club on Sundays until 3:00 p.m. and then left for home. The snack line contained leftover food from the brunch.

In 1992, I received a phone call from a friend that worked in personnel informing me that I had a line number for (E7) Master Sergeant. I had a low line number and was promoted during the first part of the promotion cycle.

I had planned earlier in my career to remain in the military for twenty-six years. The secretary of defense changed the high year of tenure for master sergeant from twenty-six years to twenty-four years. I was notified by the base personnel office airman that I could not remain in the club career field. All military club managers were being removed from the career field and were replaced with civilian managers. The reason given was that the civilian club managers would be at the bases for a longer period of time. The military club managers could receive an assignment to leave. When I was notified that I could not remain in the club field, I was given an option: I could return to the administrative career field (702X0) or work at another facility within the morale and welfare squadron. I had been working at the club in the club career field from 1989 to 1992.

I was the last active duty military club manager in all of the military branches to leave the career field. I selected the recreation center as the place I wanted to work until I retired from the military. When I reported to the recreation center, I met with the recreation center manager, and he informed me that he was placing me in charge of the food operation. I made additions to the food menu and developed a new party brochure. I was responsible for scheduling wedding receptions and parties. I met with the different people to discuss food prices and the type of setup they wanted for their function. The recreation center did not have the staff to work the parties. I contacted the club personnel to work the parties at the recreation center. The club employees that were interested in working came to the recreation center to work the parties and special functions.

Military retirees and active duty personnel came to the recreation center on Sundays to watch sports on the big-screen television. I ensured that food snacks were placed in the dining area for the customers. There were numerous customers visiting the recreation center that normally visited the club. I was informed that the customers that were at the club followed me to the recreation center when I transferred there. During the lunch period, the dining area was full to the capacity with customers. The recreation center manager and I had to assist with taking orders and cleaning tables for customers to sit. When the cook required assistance in the kitchen I gave assistance. I performed inspections of the food areas to ensure that they were clean. I had to check the dates on leftover food to ensure that it was used prior to the expired date. I was required to perform an inventory of the bar and food department at the end of each month.

During my tour at the recreation center, I was notified by the base personnel airman that I was required to go to Honduras on a temporary duty assignment. I was also informed that I had to report there on Christmas Day. I informed the personnel airman to send a message to headquarters requesting that my reporting date be changed to January 1, 1993. I received a message from headquarters informing me that I had to report on the original reporting date. Prior to being reassigned to the recreation center after my time was completed at the club, a performance report was written by my supervisor. The performance report reads as follows:

Technical Sergeant Hodge sets high standards that are the highest in the Air Force. Increased sales, coupled with increase in membership income and outstanding programs are his key success ingredients. Sales during the period increased to $353,000 and net income to $35,000 and club membership increased by 6%. During the club's $300,000 renovation project Technical Sergeant Hodge was responsible for coordinating with the contractors, relocating rooms, disposing of property, and still maintaining operations. As a result, Langley Air Force Base has one of the best facilities in the Air Force. Successful programs he has instituted include a base-wide delivery service that generated $20,000 a month in income, nightly bar bingo that generated $20,000 a month in Income and top name entertainment. His ability to manage his time, people appropriated and nonappropriated funds are unsurpassed. He is a service oriented people person whose leadership and business acumen Is respected by all. This report covered the period 12 July 1989 to 11 July 1990. The next report covers the period 12 July 1990 to 29 April 1991. The superior performance of Technical Sergeant Hodge was proven during this period of instability and change within the Noncommissioned Officers Club and the club management career field. With the congressionally mandated loss of all appropriated fund Support to clubs and the First Tactical Fighter Wing deployment to Saudi Arabia, the effect was the loss of $180,000 in appropriated fund support and the deployment of 25% of the membership. The results were that his operation remained profitable; membership satisfaction was at an all time high, and all Tactical Air Command (TAC) goals were exceeded. In spite of all major obstacles, he was able to increase sales by $35,000 and decrease expenses by $30,000 during this period. He is strong in all areas and is a tireless worker and manager. TSgt Hodge Sets the standard of excellence in club operations and then makes it happen.

The last performance report that I received at the club covered the period April 30, 1991, to April 29, 1992. During this period I sewed my E7 stripe on, and the commander and my supervisor pinned the stripe on my shoulder boards. The next performance report is as follows:

Master Sergeant Hodge's key success ingredients increased sales, increased membership and outstanding programs. Sales during this period increased $75,000, net income $25,000, and membership Six percent. He overcame the loss of $300,000 in appropriate funds support by implementing tight internal controls and excellent programs. Some programs implemented were big name entertainment, bar bingo, base wide delivery service, kiddies' nights and kiddies buffets. His knowledge of all aspects of the club business is unsurpassed and he set the standards for others to follow.

I informed my wife about the temporary duty assignment (TDY) request, and we discussed why I had to arrive in Honduras on December 25. I realized that I could not have the (TDY) cancelled. I decided that I would take the temporary duty assignment and perform the job that I was trained to do to the best of my ability. When the temporary duty orders were, published I picked up my plane tickets. I was issued a chemical suit from the base supply squadron. I packed the suit and the clothing and uniforms that I would be using in Honduras. My wife drove me to the airport on December

24, 1992, and I boarded a flight for Charleston Air Force Base in South Carolina.

When I arrived at Charleston Air Force Base, I checked into billeting and stayed overnight. I boarded A C-5 aircraft the next day for Honduras. I wore a heavy coat because the weather in Virginia and South Carolina was cold. When I arrived in Honduras, the weather was very hot, and I had to remove the jacket I was wearing. There was a military bus at the airport to transport arriving military personnel to their final destination.

When I arrived at the squadron, I was issued a pillow, two sheets, and two blankets. I was instructed to report to the hut where I would be living. I walked about one-half blocks to my living quarters. The building was a wood building sitting on wooden stakes that elevated it from the ground. The building had a tin top, and screen were in the areas where windows normally are. There were four small rooms in the building and a small area for cooking. Each room had a bed, wall locker, and a nightstand. There were portable toilets outside the buildings. The portable toilets did not have lights inside. Everyone that went to the bathroom during the night had to use a flashlight to see. The temperatures reached 116 degrees during the day and dropped to 50 degrees at night. The portable toilets were cleaned each day to keep the smell down. I arrived on the weekend, and after settling in, I decided to visit the clubs that I was responsible for.

I wore civilian clothing to prevent the employees from recognizing me. I observed the employees working in the clubs and the manner in which they performed their duties. The clubs had screens in the window slots. There were wooden tables and chairs in the clubs for the members to use. There was a jukebox in each club where the member could insert their money and select the type music to be played. There were ceiling fans in the clubs and huts to keep the troops cool. Beer and soda were the only drinks sold in the clubs. Snacks such as hot pockets and chips were also sold in the clubs. There were E-7 military members assigned to each club to perform duties as duty managers. Their duty was to keep the troops in line and resolve any problems that occurred.

On Monday morning I went to the personnel office and processed into the squadron. I was assigned to the Army unit and was required to process into the Air Force and army squadron. The army commander directed me to correct the audit that had occurred several months before I arrived there. He also directed me to set up a small commissary for the troops to purchase food. I attended the commanders' meeting after completing the in processing. He introduced me to the sergeant majors and first sergeants from the different units on base and off. He informed them that I was the new club custodian, and they could direct all club business to me. Each commander and first sergeant gave me advice on different things that should be changed in the clubs. I took each suggestion that was given to me and gave each one strong consideration. Each thing considered for change was for the support of the troops.

The first step I instituted to correct the audit was to ensure that qualified personnel were working in the clubs. The next step that I took was to order new cash registers for the club and train the personnel how to operate them. The next step was to set up an account where the employees were paid with a check and not cash. I contacted the Commissary Manager in Panama and informed him that I would be coming to Panama to discuss my commissary requirements. I developed a food list of items I wanted to sell in the commissary. I boarded a C-5 aircraft for Panama and visited the commissary manager at Howard Air Force base. I presented the list to the commissary manager and informed him what I was attempting to do. He informed me that the line items that I requested would be placed on a military flight and sent to Honduras. There were military flights that came to Honduras three times per week from Panama. The manager informed me to fax the food list to his office each time I required a food shipment. He informed me that he would have the food placed on a plane and shipped to Honduras.

I departed Panama and returned to Honduras Air Base after meeting with the commissary manager and getting the food request process set up. When I returned to Honduras, there was another challenge facing me. I had to locate a building to use for a commissary and a location for the building. I contacted the civil engineers and inquired about having them build a building. I was informed that there were two portable buildings on base, and I could have both of them. The engineer asked me where I wanted the building that was going to be used for a commissary put together. I informed him to put the building together and connect it to one of the clubs.

After one week the building was put together and connected to the club. There were coolers and food racks inside the building to store frozen foods. I used three Honduran nationals to work in the food operation. The two female employees worked as cashiers, and the male stocked the freezers and picked up the food from the airport when it arrived.

When the first shipment of food arrived, I did not pay for it right away because I had not generated funds to make the payment. I developed flyers to advertise the hours of operations and the food prices. We did not know it the first day that we opened the commissary how sales would be. When we opened the doors it seemed like everyone on base arrived to make a food purchase. We ran out of food and did not have any food items to sell for the next day. I had to develop a policy to prevent this from happening again. I placed a limit on each item an airman and solider could purchase. When the military members required more than the limit, I placed a special order with the Panama commissary. We opened the commissary three times per week for the soldiers and airmen to shop. After the limit was placed on the food items, the food supply did not become depleted. I had turned the process at the base around and all procedures were being followed. I had a bill with the commissary for $13,000 for the food. I went to the accounting and finance office and made a payment for $6,500.

The second food sale generated enough funds for me to make the payment for the other half of the money owed. This is how I paid for the food and the employees that worked for me. I attended the monthly meetings with the commanders to discuss open business items and close items that were completed. I realized that I would be there for only four months, so I began to put a training binder together for my replacement. There was a secretary that worked in my office. She received all the funds from the club managers and recounted the money when it was turned into her. She also issued money banks to the managers to use for their operation. We did not have a bank to deposit our money, so we deposited it into a safe in the office.

When I arrived in Honduras, the prior manager had gone. I did not have anyone to explain some of the problems that required correcting. I did not want to leave my replacement with the same problems that I faced when I arrived. There were dirt roads that were used for transportation. We were not permitted to leave the base unless we were on official business. We were required to have two vehicles, and each vehicle was required to have a weapon in each one.

On Saturday mornings a friend that worked in the dining facility would walk over to the barbecue barrels and start a fire. When the fire was ready, he would place a slab of ribs, hamburgers, hot dogs, and chicken on the pit. Later other military members that lived in the complex began to bring out their food items and place them on the pit. Some other military members brought out playing cards, dominos, checkers, chest games, DVD players, and other types of music. This process began on Saturday mornings and continued until Sunday nights. On numerous occasions, military members would be passing by and hear the music and noise, and they would stop and join in on the games and fun. This was a form of entertainment for the military members. There was a swimming pool and jogging track for the military members to use. On Saturday mornings we kept the commissary open all day to serve the military members. The troops and commanders were happy with the hours of operation. We did not have a bank on base, so I had to deposit the money in a safe in my office. When the cashiers opened the commissary, the secretary in my office made banks for them to use. I instructed the club managers to ensure that an inventory was performed each night after closing. The inventory had to be compared with the sales slips. When there was a shortage of ten dollars or more, the managers were required to find the mistake.

Prior to my arrival, the club managers had been bringing the deposits to the office whenever they desired. I directed them to make the deposits in my office each day no later than twelve o'clock. Honduras was a very poor country in certain areas. There were unpaved roads throughout the areas of the base. During the summer months the wind blew dust from the roads. When vehicles were driven on the roads, dust covered the vehicles and areas. There were small concessions on the base such as dry cleaners, shopette, and dining facility. The hut that I lived in was approximately one-half mile from the cleaners. I walked everywhere, so when I walked to the cleaners, my shirt would be wet from sweat.

When I arrived in Honduras, I was surprised to see the different military units there. The units there were the Army, Air Force, Navy, Marines, Coast Guard, and several special forces. The three clubs that I was responsible for was managed by military members. When I arrived, the assistant manager was managing one of the clubs. He had not been trained to manage the club. I met with the individual and asked if he wanted to continue managing the club. He informed me that he was interested in managing the club, but he did not know how. I informed him that I would train him how to complete the paperwork on all procedures in managing the club.

After several months of training, the assistant manager was placed in charge of the club. I stopped at the club each day to inquire about the club and check with the manager on club operations. He informed me that if he came into anything that he was unsure of, he would contact me. When the managers wanted equipment for the clubs or repairs accomplished, they submitted the paperwork to me. I submitted the paperwork to the club council, and the council members voted on the items. When the council gave their approval, the equipment was ordered, or the repairs were accomplished. When tables and chairs were requested, they were made on the local economy. This process was cheaper than ordering the items.

Prior to my arrival, the sergeant major had been selecting the military members to manage the clubs. After my arrival, the commander informed them that I would be selecting the managers of the clubs. All drinks purchased at the clubs had to be consumed inside the club. The clubs would normally open at 5:30 p.m. and remain open until 11:00 p.m. Mondays through Thursdays. On Fridays the clubs remained open until 1:00 a.m. I visited each club on Thursdays, Fridays, and Saturdays to observe the club operation. Sometimes I would perform a surprise cash count and inventory count. The club managers did not know that I was going to perform the cash or inventory count. When the month began on Saturdays, the inventory of the entire club was performed during the morning before the club opened for business.

When military members were on official business and had to leave the base, other military members had to accompany them. Two vehicles had to be driven, and one military member in each vehicle carried a weapon. There was an M-16 in one vehicle, and a nine millimeter in the other vehicle. Once the official business was completed, the military members had to return to the base. When my replacement arrived, I ensured that he attended the function so he could meet the other military members.

The club managers had begun to turn in their deposits on time and performed the daily inventories. I continued to use the funds generated from the commissary food sales, to pay the employees and purchase additional food to sell. There was some construction projects scheduled at the clubs that was awaiting approval from the committee. I continued to review everything involved with the club operation with my replacement until it was time for me to depart.

The base that I was TDY to was Soto Canto Air Base which is a Honduran military installation And home of the Honduran Air Force Academy. It is located ten miles from Comayagua (Population, 33,000), and some sixty miles from Tegucigalpa, the capital of Honduras. Soto Cano has been the headquarters of earlier joint task forces, and continues as the headquarters for the U.S. military presence in Honduras.

United States facilities consisted of temporary buildings (C-huts) of tropical design, constructed of wood. The enlarged airfield accommodates C-130s, C-141s, and the giant C-5 Galaxy transport aircraft. The airstrip has made Soto Cano an important link for U.S. military Air traffic in Central America. The base itself was about two miles wide and six miles long. Soto Cano AB was little more than a valley of parched soil and thick weeds prior to August 1983. After the headquarters elements of JTF-11 arrived, part of Soto Cano was transformed into first a city of tents, and later, one of austere, wooden tropical huts. The base lies in the Comayagua valley, and is ringed by 9,500 feet peaks to the east and west. There are two main Areas within Soto Cano the east side, where most of the daily operation of JTF-B occurs; and Camp Pickett, located on the west side of Soto Cano. Camp Picket is home of the 4/228th Aviation Regiment, and this is the helicopter operations area of the base.

Honduras was one of the poorest and least developed countries in Latin America. The economy was based primarily on agriculture, but there are extensive forest, marine, and mineral resources. Although unemployment officially was estimated at 10% to 15%, under-employment was much higher than, perhaps as high as 40% of the work force. The literacy rate was only about 60%. Life expectancy at birth was 63 years, while infant mortality was 60 per thousand. Honduras had one of the highest birth rates in Latin America at 5.6 per thousand. After the severe recession of the early 1980s, Honduras had achieved moderate but steady economic Growth, partly due to large U.S. economic assistance. (Soto Cano Air Base Guide JTF Bravo Pub 1.)

I continued to train my replacement and decided that it was time for me to depart. I processed out from the squadron the following week. The major and captain that I also reported to instructed, the sergeant first class to set up a going-away party for me, and I received an Achievement Award from the squadron. I said my goodbyes on Friday and flew to Charleston Air Force Base in South Carolina on Sunday morning. I stayed in billeting overnight, and the next day I flew on a commercial flight to Newport News, Virginia. When my plane landed and I walked off the plane, my wife and daughter were at the airport to meet me. The first thing that my wife asked me was, "What happened to you?"

I replied to her, "The sun." She asked me the question because my skin had become darker from the hot sun in Honduras than before I left. I was happy to be home, and I enjoyed the weekend off before reporting to work on Monday morning.

I reported to the recreation center on Monday morning and continued working on the programs that I began before I left. I started a breakfast program in the restaurant. I added several new food items to the lunch menu. Prior to the holidays, customers booked the ballroom for parties and other functions. Numerous organization employees booked their Christmas parties at the recreation center. When these parties were scheduled at night, the director and I remained at the center to ensure that the function was set up and served properly. The recreation center also provided reduced travel for military family members. The food and labor costs were very important at the recreation center. I worked closely with the director to keep the cost low. We had to ensure that the inventory was performed as accurately as possible at the end of each month. We scheduled the employees for their shifts, and when business was slow, they were sent home. When employees worked overtime, it was normally to cover a special function.

The recreation center received some appropriate support. I enjoyed working in the recreation center because the job that I performed was similar to the job performed at the club. After being at the recreation center for several weeks, I received a call from the base personnel office informing me that I had to go TDY to Florida for the Hurricane Hugo cleanup. I informed the base personnel that I was not going anywhere because I was retiring within ninety days. I continued to work at the club part-time assisting with the bingo program.

We had planned to remain in the area after I retired. I submitted my paperwork to the base personnel office for retirement. We had applied for a home loan and were waiting to hear from the loan officer. During the wait, our daughter Gloria called and informed us that she was working at night, and she did not have transportation home after work. I informed her to save money from each check to purchase tickets to use for the bus. She informed us that the bus stopped delivering passengers to different locations after certain times. When I was at work on a particular day, I decided that we were moving to California. I informed my wife about my decision to retire from the military. I went to the personnel office and completed the paperwork for retirement. I was scheduled for a physical to ensure that I was healthy. I also was scheduled for dental appointments so I could have any problems corrected. The personnel office gave briefings on finding employment after retirement. There were numerous briefings that I was required to attend for retirement. I also had to visit accounting and finance after I received my retirement orders. The finance personnel had to be notified about my retirement date.

During my preparation for retirement, I was thinking about different things. One of the most important things was going from getting paid two times per month to one time per month. When the results of the physical was received by the doctor, he had me visit his office. I explained to the doctor that I had been experiencing back pain for some time. I decided to apply for disability before I retired because the procedure was difficult to accomplish after retirement. I was issued a checklist of different agencies that I must visit to give a copy of my retirement orders. The personnel at the different agencies were also required to initial my paperwork. My wife and I began to donate different items to agencies to reduce our household weight.

On my retirement date, all my military records were required to be at the base personnel office before I could retire.

Joint Base Langley-Eustis is a United States military facility located adjacent to Hampton and Newport News, Virginia. The base is an amalgamation of the United States Air Force's Langley Air Force Base and the United States Army's Fort Eustis, which was merged on October 1, 2010.

Retirement

When I first enlisted in the military on May 29, 1969, I had not planned to remain in the military for twenty years. After the first four years were completed, I decided to remain for another four years. I enjoyed traveling to different states in the United States. I especially enjoyed traveling to different countries outside the United States. After serving in the military for eight years, I realized that I was almost at the halfway point to completing twenty years.

During the first four years of my enlistment, I wanted to become an officer in the military. I received my Associate of Science degree from Thomas Edison College, after forwarding my transcripts to them from Kittrell College. I applied for the Airman's Education Commissioning Program (AECP). The program was set up for enlisted personnel that desired to become officers in the United States Air Force. Once selected for the program, the individual would attend a university full-time. Upon completing the program and graduating, the individual would attend Officers Training School, for several weeks at Lackland Air Force Base and be commissioned as a second lieutenant.

I was accepted into the program in 1973, but Congress had been depleted of the funds, and I could not attend the program. I was really disappointed and upset when I was informed that I could not attend the program. I decided to remain in the enlisted ranks and would not pursue a commissioning program again. I decided to move as far as possible up the promotion ladder in the enlisted ranks. I completed all military courses and schools that were available to me. I reached the rank of Master Sergeant (E7) during my career. When I was promoted to Master Sergeant, the high year of tenure was twenty-six years. The secretary of defense changed the time to twenty-four years.

I requested a retirement date of June 1, 1993. I completed the paperwork for retirement, and my retirement orders were published. My retirement ceremony was set up at the noncommissioned officers club. There were numerous friends and coworkers at the ceremony. During the ceremony, I was remembering all the places I and the family had traveled to. I also thought of the many friends we had made during our travels. I remembered all the different jobs that I had performed during my career. I remembered the good times and bad times during my career.

There was one thing on my mind, and that was pay. I had been receiving a pay check every two weeks for the past twenty-four years. After I retired I would receive a check once per month. This was a little scary because I had been working for twenty-four years, and it was all coming to an end. The task that I had performed for so many years was over. I realized that I had reached a certain age in my life.

During the retirement ceremony when I was standing at the podium, all of these things were going through my mind. I also realized that even though I was retiring, I was starting a second career. During the retirement briefing I was informed that I would receive 55 percent of my base pay for retirement pay for the rest of my life. During the retirement ceremony, my wife was presented a retirement certificate for supporting me during my military career all those years. I did not really want to retire, but I was happy that I had reached one plateau in my life and was ready to start another one.

The ceremony was a beautiful ceremony, with the squadron commander presiding. He directed me to report to the front of the room at the podium, where my prior career jobs were read to the guests. Different members in the audience were given a chance to speak. The commander informed the audience about the different jobs I had performed in my career. He also informed them about the different bases that I had been stationed on during my career. He also explained about the numerous moves I had made during my career.

One of my best friends came to my retirement ceremony, Myron K. Webb. Myron and I were stationed together in Vietnam in 1971, Homestead Air Force base in 1976, and Spangdahlem Air Base in 1983. Myron and I worked part-time at several of the bases we were station on. We went to different areas in Germany and Homestead, Florida, together. Myron is a good friend, and I have known his family for a long time.

I was sad and happy to be retiring because I realized that some military members did not make it to retirement. I was sad to be leaving the many friends that I had made during my career. I was happy to be able to say I retired from the military honorable. The commander presented me with a Meritorious Service Medal with one oak leaf cluster. My friends came to the podium and congratulated me on my retirement after the ceremony ended.

RELOCATED TO SACRAMENTO

After the furniture was packed and picked up for shipping, we cleaned the house and moved into billeting on base until we departed the area. We said our goodbyes to our friends and began our drive across country. We were not in a hurry, so we stopped each night for dinner and checked into a hotel. We took pictures of different states that we drove through.

After several days of driving we arrived in Sacramento, California. We checked into billeting on McClelland Air Force Base until we located a house. We arrived in Sacramento on the weekend, and we began to search for houses and applied for employment on Monday morning. I drove my wife to different job locations to complete applications and drop off resumes. We performed this task during the morning hours. The second half of the day was used to search for houses. We remained in billeting thirty days before we located a house. We finally located a three-bedroom home with one bath, family room, kitchen, and garage. The landlord did not perform a credit check because I was retired from the military. We slept on the floor using sleeping bags because the furniture had not arrived. I went to the Morale Welfare and Recreation Squadron and signed out two sleeping carts.

When we were sleeping on the floor, our backs would become sore. We just could move around the following day after sleeping on the floor. The sleeping carts were not much better to sleep on because we would have the same pain the following morning. We continued to apply for different job openings each day. The vehicle I was driving did not have a working air conditioner. We attempted to accomplish everything we had to before the temperature went off the chart. The temperatures were normally hotter in the afternoons than the mornings.

Finally our furniture arrived, and we were rescued from the floor and sore backs. I had applied for a security job and several other jobs with different companies. The human resources personnel contacted me and informed me that I had been hired. I drove to the security company and completed the paperwork and was issued a schedule and several uniforms. I was assigned to work at a supermarket in a bad part of the city.

Each day I went to work, a police officer parked his vehicle at the store and remained there until the store closed. I was also required to walk around the store and in the parking lot checking for vehicle vandalism. I continued to apply for employment with other companies. Gloria had been hired at a clothing store in the mall. We only had one vehicle, and I drove Beulah to work each morning when I arrived at home. I changed security companies and began to work on the night shift. I also drove Gloria to work in the afternoon. Gloria had been searching for a vehicle and located a GEO Metro. I cosigned for her, and she purchased the vehicle. This eliminated me from driving Gloria to work, and gave me more time to concentrate on applying with other companies.

Gloria came home one day and asked me about army recruiters in the area. I informed her that there were recruiters in the area. Several weeks later she informed us that she had enlisted into the army. She departed for training several weeks later and was in the army for four years.

I decided that I required a job that paid me more money. I applied for an account manager's job at a rental company. I went to the store and interviewed with the store manager. I was hired and began to train as an account manager. I was responsible for managing thirty customer accounts. After completing the required training at the store, I was also responsible for other duties. I assisted potential customers with completing paperwork to obtain new accounts. When the customer's account became one to fourteen days late for their payments, I called and mailed letters to them. I was always attempting to get a commitment from the customer stating when they would make a payment on their account. When the accounts became fifteen days past due, I was responsible for retrieving the merchandise from the customer. When the customers decided to bring their accounts current by making the correct payment, I accepted it.

On Mondays through Saturdays from eight to nine in the morning, I phoned customers who were late on making their payments. I was required to get a commitment from the customers stating what date and time they would make their payments. When the store opened on Saturday mornings, I drove the store vehicle to the customers' homes to collect past due payments.

I would stay on the road sometimes five and six hours attempting to collect past due payments and merchandise. I would return to the store after making the run and work on increasing store sales. I was required to maintain the account credit at the store requirement.

When new merchandise arrived at the store, I ensured that it was added to the store inventory list. Each store had a credit and sales goal that had to be obtained each week. The credit and sales goal started over each week with a new goal. I decided to change jobs because I was unhappy performing the job. Some of the customers could not afford to rent the property from the rental store. One part of the job that I did not enjoy was going to the customer's home demanding a payment or the merchandise. The main reason that I ended my employment with the company was due to the store manager placing me in a life-threatening situation with a customer. On the day that the incident occurred, I returned to the store and informed the manager that I quit.

The next job that I obtained was in the same line of work. This time around I was a store manager trainee. I began as an account manager and performed the same duties that I had previously performed. I could not train in the store that I was working in. Some of the subjects that I trained on were customer service, sales, store credit, merchandising, pricing, inventory, and deliveries. During the training period, I assisted other account managers with their accounts. When customers came to the store, I accepted payments and posted the payments to their accounts.

Each week all trainees were given a test and were required to make 70 percent. There were twelve to fourteen different tests that I was required to take and pass before I could become a store manager. I did not pass all the tests I was given, so I could not become a store manager. I left the store and searched for other employment with a different company. I received a notification to come in for an interview. During the interview, I completed the paperwork, and a background check was performed. I was offered a position with the ABZ security company.

I arrived at the company on Monday morning and met with the supervisor at the security company. I had met with the operation manager earlier and informed him that I wanted to work Mondays through Fridays. The operations manager had informed the supervisor that I wanted to work a day shift Mondays through Fridays. The supervisor informed me that he did not have a Monday through Friday day-shift schedule. I began to train on each shift that was available.

After working several weeks training, I received a call from the day-shift supervisor informing me that he had an opening on day shift Mondays through Fridays available. I began to work Mondays through Fridays from 4:30 a.m. to 2:30 p.m. When I arrived for my shift, my supervisor escorted me to my duty station and introduced me to my coworkers. I began working in a warehouse lobby area that was in a restricted area. Everyone that entered the warehouse area was required to have an access badge or be escorted by someone with a badge. The officer that I was replacing trained me for one week before he left.

Several weeks after I began to work at the post a metal detector, and a rapiscan machine was installed in the lobby entrance. There were computer chips in the warehouse, that I was responsible for preventing from being removed without the proper paper work. Each employee was required to enter and exit through the metal detector and not set the alarm off. They were required to remove their shoes, belts, jewelry, underwire bras, and change from their pockets. When the employees could not go through the detector without causing the alarm to sound, their manager was contacted, and he arrived at the detector to escort them. I also inspected all equipment that was removed from the area to ensure that a property pass accompanied the equipment. Employees entering the area with cameras were required to have the camera pass approved and signed by the manager. When they arrived without a camera pass, I held the camera in the lobby until they returned. I inspected all hand carried items to ensure that they were free of company property. Each employees' shoes had to be sent through the x-ray machine after they were removed.

A shift supervisor's position opened several years later. I applied for the position, but I was not selected. The selection process was unfair, and the most qualified candidate was not selected. I wrote a letter to the area manager and informed her about the selection process. She arrived the following week and conducted an investigation into the selection process. The branch and human resource managers did not know that I had written the letter. Several weeks later the branch manager was removed from the position. I worked at different posts for a short time before I was assigned to another lobby. I remained there and continued to work for several years.

My job in the lobby consisted of issuing one hundred badges to employees arriving each morning. I also checked property being removed for property passes. I was also responsible for collecting employee badges at the end of their shift and filing them in containers. A new site was being constructed in Woodland, California, and there were supervisory positions open to employees that were interested. I was contacted by the operations manager about applying for the day-shift supervisor position. I applied for the position and was selected to fill the opening.

I drove out to the site and met with the operation manager. He explained his expectations of each supervisor. He was the first line supervisor for all the supervisors. The site was located approximately thirty minutes driving time from my home. The operations manager was a retired highway patrolman. He was a very good supervisor, and he was always concerned about the officers' welfare.

On my first day at the site after meeting with the manager, he informed me that there were three warehouses with roll-up doors that had to be secured. There were doors that did not have locks, so we had to purchase temporary locks until we received permanent locks from the company. I began to develop operating instructions that pertained to the operation of the site. The next step involved obtaining sign-in sheets for the officers to sign in on each shift to receive their pay. Standard operating instructions were developed for the truck gate that all deliveries were made through.

There were six buildings on the site, and three were operational. Some of the other things I was responsible for were writing performance reports, counseling employees, and safety. The three non-operational buildings were being worked on after we moved into the first three. Cameras were installed in the buildings, and the fire system was tested daily. I trained the officers on my shift, and some on the other shifts. The majority of the officers on my shift were senior citizens. I did not worry about the officers on my shift reporting late or not reporting. The supervisors on the other two shifts were always concerned about their employees' work ethics. When employees did not report for their scheduled shift, it was difficult to get officers from other sites to come to work at the site. The site was thirty to forty-five minutes of driving for some officers. Some officers could not afford to buy gas for their vehicle if they came to the site for more than one shift.

On numerous occasions when an officer did not report to work, I would be forced to cover the shift with overtime. The site operated three shifts that consisted of days, swings, and graves. I had to ensure that each officer attended the CPR/first aid classes because it was a requirement to work at the site. We were responsible for administering first aid and CPR to coworkers and client employees when required.

I developed post orders for each post. The post orders were placed at each post, and a copy was maintained in the office. The post orders gave instructions on how to operate the post. I coordinated security issues and policies concerning the company employees with the client. The client manager was receptive and ensured that all employees followed the regulations. Whenever a problem occurred with client employees I contacted the company manager. He would address the problem immediately, and a solution would be decided upon in a short period of time. When the three additional buildings became operational, the same number of posts were set up as in the original buildings. When the employees began to arrive at building 1, they began the forty-hour training program. They were not permitted to begin working until they completed forty hours of training.

There was a safety coordinator on the site responsible for taking care of emergencies. I had to respond to the emergencies with the safety coordinator. Once the buildings were operational, tractor trailers began to arrive with merchandise to be stored in the buildings. The gate officers were responsible for processing trucks into the site and empty trailers out the site. When the officer was very busy, I went to the gate on different occasions to assist the gate officers. There was an officer that performed rover patrols. He was always available to assist the gate officers when required. I assigned two officers at the gate when we received information that a large number of trucks were arriving at the site. The trucks arrived at the site twenty-four hours per day. More vehicles arrived at the site during the day and swing shifts. When the trucks arrived, they were inspected to ensure that the seals on the trailers were sealed. This procedure insured that the entire product arrived at the site and was not tampered with. New seals were placed on the vehicles before they departed the site.

I continued to work at the site as the day-shift manager for several years. I was responsible for meeting the new officers and briefing them about the site. I had to ensure that they were trained properly before placing them on a post alone. I was responsible for submitting the sign in sheets to the main office. Each officer was informed to always work safely. When the officers arrived at the site for the first time, I ensured that they were issued a picture identification and entry badge.

My work schedule at the site was Mondays through Fridays 5:30 a.m. to 1:30 p.m. I also worked on a second job at a different location. The work schedule on the second job was 3:00 p.m. to 10:00 p.m. Sometimes I was required to work overtime on the second job. I did not arrive at home until approximately 3:30 a.m. I did not sleep when this occurred because I had to report to the security site at 5:30 a.m. I would normally come home and change my clothes and go to my first job.

The supervisors at the second job informed me that I was doing a good job. I was responsible for operating a machine. I had to process a specific number of items during my shift. When I worked, I wrote the number of items I processed into a notebook during my shift. On the eighty-ninth day of employment, my direct supervisor left instruction with another supervisor to terminate my employment. When the supervisor informed me about the termination, I did not say anything because I knew what I had to do. I gave him my badge and walked out the building. The next day, I contacted the EEOC and filed a grievance against the agency. I visited numerous lawyers, and they reviewed my paperwork and stated that I had a good case. After years of going back and forth with paperwork, a judge instructed the agency and I to settle out of court.

Several weeks later we settled out of court, and I was given an opportunity to return to the company. During this time I gave up my shift manager's job at the security company. I returned to the security company later and was hired in a part-time position. After working several weeks in the part-time position, I informed the supervisor that I needed a full-time position. The supervisor informed me that he would review the schedule for open positions. I was given a full-time position a week later, and all was good.

Several months later, I was offered a supervisor position, and I accepted the position. I was responsible for training all lobby personnel. I interviewed candidates for open positions and made selections to fill those positions. I was responsible for writing performance reports and counseling letters when required. I had to inspect the officers each day to ensure that their appearance was presentable. I recommended personnel for awards and promotion to higher-paying positions. I ensured that new policies and procedures were submitted to each lobby and put into effect. I visited different lobbies when new changes occurred to discuss the changes with each officer. Some officers did not accept changes without disagreeing with the change.

One day I was working, and my manager informed me that a shift manager position was opening at a different site. He informed me to think about applying for the position. I was informed that the position was salaried and on the grave shift. The supervisor also informed me that he required my answer in two days, if I was interested in the position. I did not want to work on the grave shift, but I had to consider the advantages of the new job. The pay at the new job was more, and the benefits were better. I discussed the new job with my wife and decided to accept the position. I informed my manager that I would accept the position; he informed me to visit the human resource manager to inquire about the position.

When I met with the human resource manager, I was given an acceptance letter that explained the pay and the job requirements. When I completed reading the information, I signed the acceptance letter and returned the letter to her. I reported to the site on Monday morning and started training with another shift manager. After several days of training, I began working on the night shift from 10:00 p.m. to 6:00 a.m. Mondays to Fridays. There were five officers assigned to my shift. My job consisted of scheduling, training, safety, writing performance reports, counseling, and interviewing. I was responsible for ensuring that the client received support from the security team.

There were six warehouses that had merchandise stored inside. There was security post inside each warehouse. There was a metal detector in the first set of buildings and one in the second set of buildings. The employees and officers were required to go through the detectors and not set the alarm off. There were officers that worked at the detectors to ensure, that employees and officers cleared through the detectors when entering and exiting the building.

I was enrolled in the Master of Arts program at the University of Phoenix during that time. I attended classes from 6:00 p.m. to 9:00 p.m. and reported to work after classes from 9: 30 p.m. to 6:00 a.m. I wrote performance reports on each officer once each year. When the report was prepared, I discussed the report with each officer and explained the rating process. Sometimes the officers did not agree with the rating they received. I always had documents to support the rating that was given.

The site was confined inside a wire fence that prevented unauthorized people from entering the site. I enjoyed being the shift manager for the site. I had to become adjusted to working at night. I would become sleepy at three each morning, and I would get up and walk through the warehouses. I also drove the security vehicle to the second set of buildings and checked the security gates. The procedure made me stay awake. When I returned to the office, it was time for me to end my shift. I also had to ensure that each officer remained awake during the shift to perform their job. We had a good team at the site, and everyone performed their job to standards. I met with the client occasionally to discuss new company requirements and changes. Each officer worked a forty-hour workweek, and I ensured that overtime was maintained at a minimum. Whenever an officer called off for his scheduled shift, I used another officer to fill the open shift. The officers were required to ensure that employees were cleared to enter different areas within the warehouse.

I continued to work at the site as the shift manager for several years. A shift manager's position became available at another site, and I informed my manager that I was interested. I was given the position and started working on the day shift as the shift supervisor. After being there for several weeks, I was informed by my manager that he was changing me to the swing shift. His reason for making the change was there was a manager with more computer experience than I. I continued to perform my duties to the best of my abilities. The client informed me that he planned to install a metal detector in the building. I contacted my manager and informed him of the client request. Two detectors were shipped to the site, and one was installed in each lobby.

I obtained a copy of the rules and policies from my previous site to aid the officers with their training. I also trained the officers on the policies and procedures pertaining to the operations of the detectors. The post orders for each post was posted at the site and was being used by the officers. Each post order was required to be reviewed on their anniversary date. Changes had to be made to the post orders to update them when they were outdated. I was responsible for the operation of the site. I had to ensure that each officer performed their duties in an acceptable and effective manner. When a new officer arrived on site, they were assigned with an officer at each post to train and learn how to work on the post. I was responsible for the success or failure of that officer. Each week I made the schedule and printed a copy for the site. The majority of the officers lived in the local area and volunteered to work overtime when required. Some of the officers lived in other cities, and during the rainy season they had problems driving to the site. During the rainy season when there was a large downpour, the streets flooded in some areas. The officers driving to the site did not realize the lanes were flooded until they attempted to drive through the water. They did not know how deep the water was until they drove into it. Sometimes they would be forced to turn around and return to their homes or attempt to reach the site from a different direction.

I had been experiencing blurred vision in my eyes. When I drove at night and I approached an exit sign, sometimes the sign was difficult for me to read. When I was making a turn and there was a curve, I ran over the curve. My wife would always inform me that I could not see. I eventually went to my family doctor and explained that I had blurred vision in my eyes. He scheduled me for a visit with an eye doctor. I went to the eye doctor, and he examined my eyes and informed me that my eyes were good. I returned to my family doctor and informed him of the results from the eye doctor. I also informed him that I continued to have the same problem. He informed me that he was sending me back to the same office, but I would be examined by a different doctor.

When I returned to the eye clinic, I was examined by a different doctor. After his examination, he informed me that he was sending me to get a MRI. I visited a facility where I was given an MRI, and I was informed that the doctor would receive the results within a few days. When the doctor received the results, he phoned me to come into the office.

When I visited his office, he informed me that I had a pituitary tumor that was pressing down on my optical nerve. This was causing me to have blurred vision. He informed me that the tumor would need to be removed by a special doctor. I was at home watching the television, and the best brain surgeon in the area was on discussing different surgeries he performed. I was referred to the same hospital where he performed his surgery. My wife and I went to the hospital and were sitting in the office waiting to see a doctor. The doctor that I had seen on television entered the room and explained that he was my doctor. He explained to my wife and me that he did not want to cut me to remove the tumor. He explained that he would remove the tumor through my nostrils by pulling it out.

I was scheduled for the surgery at 6:00 a.m. on a Monday. I remember being in the room, to receive all the shots to put me to sleep and numb the area where the tumor would be removed. I was instructed to count from number ninety back to one. When I opened my eyes, half the tumor had been removed, and I was in the recovery room. I had splints in my nose, and my feet were strapped to the bed. I was in the intensive care room for several hours. I was then placed in a room where I could have visitors. The nurse asked if I wanted any medicine for pain, and I informed her that I did not need any. I had asked God to take away all the pain. One of the nurses was a born-again believer, and she understood why I did not need pain medicine. The nurses that were not born again did not understand. I remained in the hospital for one day and was released to go home. I was scheduled for the second surgery a month later and went through the same experience. The doctor had planned to go through the same incision that he used for the first surgery. He discovered that the incision had healed, and he was shocked. He had to make a second incision to perform the tumor removal.

When I recovered from the tumor removal, my eyesight was clearer than it had ever been. I had purchased eyeglasses prior to the surgery when my vision was blurred. I returned the glasses to the store and received the money back that I had paid for the glasses. Several months prior to my tumor removal, I became thirsty and was running to the bathroom every five minutes. My wife informed me to make an appointment with my doctor. When I visited the doctor, I informed him about my symptoms. He sent me to the laboratory to get a blood test. After the test was administered, the doctor received the results and contacted me and informed me to come to his office. When I arrived at the doctor's office, he informed me that I had diabetes, and he prescribed medications for me. The medication was supposed to control the diabetics. I had to make a decision if I wanted to continue to live with the diabetics for the rest of my life. Exercise and eating the right foods are the things that have controlled the diabetics.

I have begun to walk for thirty minutes each day. I had to decide to stop eating the foods that is turned into sugar when eaten by a diabetic. I have to visit the doctor every three months and the laboratory. My feet are also checked for circulation and nerve damage. Diabetes affects the following organs: eyes, kidney, and feet. I also have my eyes checked every three months. The medication is taken two times per day. I also pray to God every day to heal me of the diabetes. I went on the Internet and found a list of foods that diabetics should eat and avoid. I check my blood sugar each day and keep track of it. I also carry hard candy in my pockets everywhere I go to eat if my blood sugar drops. Sometimes in the morning when I wake up, my blood sugar is lower than it should be. I am required to drink orange juice or eat anything sweet to make it come back up. I drink diet sodas but have been advised that the diet sodas are not good for a diabetic. I am also required to keep my feet clean and dry. My wife cut my toenails to prevent the large toenails from growing into my toes. My brother Howard is also a diabetic, and I do not know of any other family member having diabetes. My daughter and sister and other brother have been tested and are not infected. My goal is to be completely free of diabetics by exercising and to get off the medication. Listed below are my blood sugar readings for the first two months when I was diagnosed with diabetes:

15 May 2001- Time: 1:25 Reading – 76 1 June 2001 – Time: 8am- Reading - 147 16 May 2001- Time: 4:30 Reading – 101 2 June 2001 – Time: 11pm- Reading - 145 May 2001- Time: 5am – Reading: 91 3 June 2001 – Time: 11pm - Reading - 129 18 May 2001- Time: 5am – Reading: 81 4 June 2001 – Time: 0820pm- Reading- 146 19 May 2001- Time: 5am – Reading: 88 5 June 2001 – Time: 11:00pm –Reading - 120 20 May 2001- Time: 5am – Reading: 100 6 June 2001 – Time: 5:00 – Reading - 110 21 May 2001- Time: 5am – Reading: 100 7 June 2001 – Time: 11:00pm – Reading: 129 22 May 2001- Time: 1:30 – Reading: 108 8 June 2001 – Time: 5:30pm – Reading: 104 23 May 2001 – Time: 5:25pm–Reading: 98 9 June 2001 – Time: 11:00pm – Reading: 173 24 May 2001 – Time: 7am – Reading: 98 10 June 2001 – Time: 11:00pm – Reading: 185 25 May 2001–Time: 6:30am –Reading: 146 11 June 2001 – Time: 1:15 – Reading: 81 26 May 2001–Time: 0430am–Reading: 86 12 June 2001 – Time: 3:45 – Reading: 112 27 May 2001 – Time: 5am Reading: 95 13 June 2001 – Time: 7:00 – Reading: 128 28 May 2001 – Time: 1105 – Reading: 151 14 June 2001 – Time: 0500 are Reading: 87 29 May 2001 – Time: 1100 – Reading: 128 15 June 2001 – Time: 0500am – Reading: 130 30 May 2001 – Time: 5pm – Reading: 134 16 June 2001 – Time: 0500am – Reading: 120 31 May 2001 – Time: 6pm – Reading: 106 17 June 2001 – Time: 0500am Reading:

79 18 June 2001 – Time: 0700 – Reading: 142 19 June 2001 – Time: 0655 – Reading: 128 2001 – Time: 0700 – Reading: 162 21 June 2001 – Time: 0650 – Reading: 144 22 June 2001 – Time: 0630 – Reading: 91 23 June 2001 – Time: 0430 – Reading: 96 24 June 2001 – Time: 2230 – Reading: 162 25 June 2001 – Time: 0545 – Reading: 109 26 June 2001 – Time: 0500 – Reading: 79 27 June 2001 – Time: 0500 – Reading: 76 28 June 2001 – Time: 0500 Reading: 96 29 June 2001 – Time: 0500 – Reading: 114

When we arrived in Sacramento, California, my wife and I was searching for a church home to attend. After visiting several churches, we settled on Calvary Christian Center. After my wife and I joined the church, we attended classes for a specific amount of time. When we completed the classes, I volunteered to be an usher, and my wife became a greeter. I arrived at church every Sunday morning and began to set each post up and place offering envelopes out. I contacted each usher prior to service so they would not be late reporting to church. We were also responsible for ensuring that the pastor was escorted to his office when he arrived. The ushers seated the members and guests when they arrived for service. We had to ensure that all seats in the sanctuary were filled starting from the front to the back of the church. Several ushers were placed in the parking lot to direct the members and guests when they arrived for service. We attended funerals and gave our assistance to the families.

During the healing services, we formed a line at the front of the sanctuary to catch the members before they fell to the floor. When a special guest speaker arrived at the church, we were responsible for providing assistance to the speaker. We also provided the speakers staff assistance when they were in attendance.

During the offering we collected the funds and placed them in the vault. When a member or guest was late turning in their offering, we accepted it and dropped it into the vault. Visitors that gave their life to Christ were given some reading material by the ushers. We escorted the new members to an empty room and explained to them what had just happened in their lives. We also explained what they must continue to do as new believers. My wife and I were members at Calvary Christian Center for twelve years before we left. The pastor called my wife and I to the front of the sanctuary one Sunday Morning and informed the members that he released us to leave.

I continued to work at the site for several years before moving to another site at a different location. In 2005, my wife went to Atlanta, Georgia, to attend the MegaFest. I informed her to purchase a newspaper while she was there and bring it home when she returned. When she returned, she gave me the newspaper, and I read through the paper and decided to request delivery of the paper each week. I reviewed the newspapers to check the housing prices and the job market in Atlanta, Georgia. After reviewing several newspapers for approximately one week, I discovered that the houses were inexpensive. I contacted a real estate office and spoke to a real estate officer. I informed the realtor that I was searching for a home. I gave the realtor the house size, location, and the price range we could afford. She began to search for the home that fit the category we required. She also put me in contact with a loan officer that she had previously sent customers to for home loans. When I contacted the loan officer, she faxed the loan paperwork to me. My wife and I completed the paperwork and faxed it back to her a few days later.

Several weeks later the loan officer contacted me and stated that we had been approved for a $120,000 loan. The realtor contacted us and requested that we fly to Atlanta so she could show us some homes in our price range. We flew to Atlanta, Georgia, in December 2005 and landed at the airport. We rented a vehicle and drove to Covington, Georgia, and checked into a hotel. The next morning we contacted the realtor and informed her where we were staying. She came to the hotel and picked us up and showed us several homes in different areas. We were not interested in any homes that we visited. The realtor drove through an area not listed with her. We noticed a home we were interested in walking through. Our realtor called the realtor listed on the For Sale sign and informed her that we wanted to walk through the home. The realtor informed our realtor that she could show us the home.

The home had four bedrooms and three bathrooms. The home also had a garage and was built in 2003, and no one had lived in the home. The selling price was $122,000, and the realtor informed us to make an offer. We made an offer of $120,000, and the offer was accepted based on us closing by a specific date. We returned to California and began to plan our move to Covington, Georgia.

We returned to Covington Georgia in January 2006 to close on the house. The realtor had not informed us of the required amount of money we needed to bring to the closing. The following morning, the realtor came to the hotel and picked us up, and we drove to the lawyer's office. When we arrived at the lawyer's office, the lawyer went through approximately one hundred pages of paperwork before coming to The end. When we completed signing all the paperwork, the lawyer informed us that we had to pay $1,600. We did not have the money to close on the house. We contacted my sister-in-law in Arkansas, and she wired us the money for closing. We paid the lawyer the money and returned to California, and I contacted ABF about their moving procedures.

The moving company employee informed me that the charge for the use of the trailer would be based on the amount of space used. The ABF driver would deliver a trailer to our home and drop it. We were responsible for loading the trailer. After my wife and I packed the household goods, we contacted ABF to deliver the trailer. We used two days to load the trailer and ensured everything was packed secure. When the trailer was completely loaded and packed, I placed the door seal inside the trailer. I called the ABF office to pick up the trailer from our home. I placed a lock on the trailer after it was completely loaded. The date the trailer was picked up was February 2006. When the driver arrived to pick up the trailer, I removed the lock, and he checked the trailer to ensure that the furniture was secure and could not move. The truck driver gave me a copy of the paperwork and drove away with the furniture. We moved into a hotel after the furniture was picked up so we could clean the house. We gave away numerous items and threw away others. We drove to a vehicle rental company, and a trailer was hooked to my truck. I drove my wife's car onto the trailer and secured it to the trailer.

Gloria and Clifford were at the rental company to say goodbye. We also had the rear end of the truck packed and began our drive to Covington, Georgia. We had a good drive coming to Georgia. We stopped at a hotel overnight and began our trip the following day. We stopped for breakfast and filled the vehicle with gas and continued on the trip. When we arrived in Louisiana, it was raining, and we stopped at a convenience store to purchase a cover to place over the items in the truck. When we arrived in Covington, Georgia, we moved into our new home, and my wife decided to repaint the rooms in different colors. I contacted the ABF office and informed the representative that we were at the Covington addresses and requested a delivery date. The ABF trailer was delivered to our home a few days later. When the trailer was delivered to our home, we began to unload the furniture. After we unloaded the trailer, I contacted the ABF office to have the trailer picked up. When the driver arrived, I paid for the furniture delivery with a certified check.

My wife and I filled out job applications and submitted résumés to different agencies for employment. I was finally hired by the Securitas security company. I was sent to a retail department store to interview with the assistant store manager. I also met the security officer that was employed at the store. After the interview I was contacted one week later and informed to report to the store the following day.

When I arrived at the store, I was introduced to the manager and department associates. I was introduced to my supervisor and coworkers at the store. The position at the store was an unarmed security position. I was responsible for preventing customers from removing merchandise from the store unless it was paid for. I was trained in the camera room where the cameras monitored the store area. I trained for approximately forty hours before I could work a shift. There was always two security officers in the store at all times.

Once I began to work, when the camera room officer observed a suspect concealing merchandise, he contacted me on the floor. He gave me a description of the suspect and the merchandise he/ she had concealed. I would approach the suspect and inform him/ her to accompany me to the manager's office on the second floor. We had to keep the suspect in eye contact, and the camera room officer had to monitor the suspect until we arrived at the office. The store manager would normally enter the office and ask the suspect if they had any merchandise on them that the store owned. When the suspect stated the truth, sometimes the store manager would not call the police department. When the police department was called, they arrived and took the suspect to jail.

I worked at the store for twelve months and more females were apprehended for shoplifting than males. I worked in the camera room for several hours each day and on the floor for the remainder of the shift. We normally worked on the floor for a specific time and then rotated to the camera room. The store manager did not want the security officers standing in one spot. He wanted us to continue to walk through the store. There was one officer on the floor some days and two officers on Fridays, Saturdays, and Sundays. We chased shoplifters on numerous occasions, and some were caught, and some escaped. The camera room officer had to ensure that the shoplifters were recorded committing a crime, before they could be stopped. I did not enjoy performing this type of job, but I continued to work there until we moved away. There were more people that moved there from other states and different countries.

The traffic in Covington and Atlanta was very congested during the early-morning and late afternoon hours. When there was an accident on the freeways it was difficult to get to work. Accidents on the freeways caused the traffic to stop, and it was impossible to bypass the accidents unless you were at an exit. When there was an alternate route around the accidents, it was possible to get to work. My wife's job was approximately twenty minutes from our home. She did not have to drive on the freeway to get to work. I had to drive for approximately twenty minutes to get to my job. I had to drive on the freeway to get to my job. The people drove very fast and unsafe for the road conditions. There were daily accidents involving big rigs and vehicles. When we had to drive through Atlanta for a long distance on the freeways, Beulah would not drive.

She began working at a retail store placing magazines and cards on racks and into slots. She was also required to move heavy bins loaded with books, from the loading docks to the front of the store. Truck-driving jobs were in high demand more than other jobs. I did not have truck-driving experience, so I did not apply for a driving position. I have a security background, and this is the area that I concentrated on. I have a bachelor and master's degree and considered a teaching career. I was required to be certified in the state before I could qualify to teach. I could not afford to be unemployed for a long period of time, so I applied for a security position. Everyone that worked in the security industry were required to have a background check.

There were some good things that occurred during the time we were living in Georgia. I had a doctor's appointment during the entire summer months. I went to visit the eye doctor, foot doctor, and the neurologist. I was also required to visit my family doctor every ninety days to have blood drawn. The blood was drawn by a lab technician who tested the blood and sent the results to the doctor. I was also required to go to the imaging department to get a picture of my head taken. The doctor wanted to monitor the area where the tumor had previously been located. I was informed by the diabetes doctor that I had a cyst on my kidney. I also ensured that I received a physical when required.

My wife and I did not like living in Georgia, and we began to plan to move to Houston, Texas. My wife's sister and her family lived in Houston, Texas. We also have a daughter that lives in Houston, Texas. She had been experiencing some problems, and we decided to move there to help her get her life back on track. I really wanted to go back to California and bypass Houston, Texas. We decided on a date to leave Georgia and began to save money for the move. Beulah circled the date that we planned to leave on the calendar. We continued to work each day and planned the move.

I contacted the ABF company to get a quote for the cost to move our household goods to Houston, Texas. I began to pick up boxes from the store where I worked. There was a stack of boxes in the garage that we used in the move from California. Beulah and I began to pack boxes and tape them for the move. Beulah and I decided on a date that we would move. We packed all the merchandise that could be packed. We gave some items to charity agencies to reduce the amount of items we possessed. I contacted the ABF office and informed the representative the date we wanted the trailer delivered.

Finally ABF delivered the trailer to our home. Beulah and I began to load the trailer during the weekdays. We took several days to load the merchandise on to the truck. I placed the seal inside the trailer to prevent the merchandise from moving. I also placed a lock on the trailer to secure the merchandise inside the trailer. I contacted the ABF office and informed the representative to send a driver to pick up the trailer. A driver came to our home to pick up the trailer, and he inspected the trailer to ensure that it was sealed. He also gave me some paperwork that listed the household goods. He drove away with the trailer on his drive to Houston, Texas. We stayed in the house the night before we departed for Texas.

The next morning we drove to a rental agency and had a trailer hooked to the truck. I drove Beulah's vehicle on to the trailer. The rental employees secured the vehicle by placing straps to the front end and back of the vehicle. After the vehicle was secured to the trailer we began our drive to Houston, Texas.

Before we left Covington, Beulah went on the Internet and searched for rental homes. We also reviewed newspapers for rental properties. We also contacted our daughter to search for homes for rent and send us the information. When a home was located, we were put in contact with the landlord. We spoke to him about the home he had for rent and the monthly cost. Beulah informed our daughter Gloria and her sister to visit the home and perform a walk through. After they completed the walk through, the landlord was contacted and informed that we were interested in renting the home. The landlord faxed the lease paperwork for our signatures. We sent the deposit to our daughter to give to the landlord. When we received the lease paperwork, we signed the papers and faxed them back to the landlord. We had a good drive from Covington, Georgia to Houston, Texas.

My wife wanted fast food one night, and I drove up to the speaker to order the food. I could not go through the drive-through because I had a trailer attached to the truck with a vehicle on it. I parked the vehicle and walked inside and picked up the food. We ate our food in the truck and then continued on our trip. We ran into rain showers as we drove closer to Houston. We stopped at a retail store and purchased a cover and placed it over the back of the vehicle. We arrived in Houston, Texas, during the late night. We drove to the home and removed our suitcases from the truck and placed them inside the house. Gloria had placed her air mattress in the house for us to use until we received our household goods. We had a goodnight's sleep overnight.

The next day we awoke, and I removed my wife's vehicle from the trailer. I drove to the rental company and returned the trailer. The drive from Covington, Georgia, to Stafford, Texas, covered approximately 950 miles. We picked up a newspaper to review for job listings. I located several security companies, and I decided to complete an application with them. The first company that I completed an application at scheduled me for an interview after several weeks. After I completed the interview, I did not hear from the human resources department until I called to ask if I had been selected for the position. I was not selected for the open position, so I went to another security company and completed an application. After several weeks the background investigation was completed, and I was scheduled to go to the office to complete additional paperwork. I was scheduled to attend class Mondays through Fridays for two weeks. I would be required to pass a test with a 70 percent passing score. I was also given a class on firearms and how to clean and safely use the weapon. When I completed the last day of class, I went to the firing range and fired the .38 pistol and the shotgun. I was required to qualify with the firearm before I could work in an armed position with the company. After I qualified with the weapon the paperwork was submitted to the state for my commissioned license. The state took one month before sending the license to me. I had to work in an unarmed position until I received my license.

I was assigned to a strip mall from 2: 00 p.m. to 10:00 p.m. Saturdays through Wednesdays. My duties required me to walk through the mall areas checking for unauthorized people. I also watched patrons in the mall and ensured that they were not harmed. During the hot summer days, I stopped at the ice cream shop for water and ice cream. There was a convenient store located on the back side of the mall. When several customers entered the store at night, the owner became nervous and called me to come to the store. I went to his store several times during my shift to ensure that he was okay. Sometimes during my shift on Saturdays, I went to the bank to get money for the store owner. During my patrols through the mall I checked each store for any unusually activity. There was a grocery store in the mall where my schedule and sign-in sheets were maintained. A policeman came to the store on Thursdays through Saturdays. He worked at the grocery store, and I would stop there to talk with him. The mall was located in a bad area of the city. Some of the store owners gave the policeman and I free sodas when we were working at the mall.

After working at the mall for one month, I was notified that my commissioned license had arrived at the office. I was scheduled to visit the branch office to be reassigned to another post. When I arrived at the office the operations officer informed me that I would be working at different post. I informed him that I preferred to work at one location during a forty-hour week. I picked up my uniforms, weapon, and ammunition from the office. I was driving to different locations each night to work. I was instructed to go to a drugstore to work, and it was located too far from my home. I informed the captains and director that I wanted to work at a post near my home. Eventually I was assigned to a post for forty hours per week at a CVS drugstore. The post was located in a bad area, and the time that I worked was from 10:00 p.m. to 6:00 a.m. Sundays through Thursdays.

I knew that I did not plan to perform the security work for a long period of time. I was continuously searching for other employment with a different company. I always ensured that I purchased the Sunday newspaper to search for employment and on the Internet. When I was reviewing the newspaper, I saw an opening for an account manager with a security company. I applied for the position and was contacted to come to the office for an interview. When I arrived for the interview, the vice president of the company conducted the interview. I gave him a copy of my résumé for his review. After the interview, he informed me that he was interviewing other applicants, and I would be contacted.

After one week I was contacted by the human resources representative, and he informed me to come for a second interview. When I arrived for the second interview, the vice president interviewed me again. He informed me that the human resources office staff would contact me during the week. Several days later the representative from the humans resources office called me and made an offer, and I accepted. I was offered a position in Texas City as an account manager at an oil company. I could not officially take the position until I had passed the safety class. I was also given a drug test and had to wait for the results to be received in the security office.

When I arrived at the office that I would be working in, my supervisor was there, and he gave me paperwork to take a second drug test. When I returned to the office, my supervisor was there, and he remained there for several weeks training me. He had also hired an officer from the site and promoted her to second lieutenant. She was my assistant and would be managing the schedule. There was a director and security manager at the site for the ISSC company. I was responsible for a six-million-dollar account per year. The director of security had his expectations as well as the security manager for me to accomplish. I also had requirements to meet with the ISSC security company. I asked my supervisor what time I should arrive at the office. He informed me that he arrives at 6:00 am each day Mondays to Fridays. I always ensured that I was at the office when he arrived.

One of the most important topics at the site was employee safety. I was given a company vehicle to drive. My drive from home was forty-five to sixty minutes during good weather. I also was given a credit card to use for gas. Normally I filled the vehicle with gas before I left the site. When I first arrived at the office, I began the day by reviewing emails and replying to those requiring a reply. When an officer on the day shift had called off, I also had to attempt to fill the post right away. Sometimes I could not fill the post with an officer that was off duty. I would go to the schedule to find out who was off and wanted to work. There was always an officer wanting to work overtime. Sometimes I had to hold an officer over that had completed a night shift to cover a day-shift post.

I ensured that all the officers were informed about important facts going on at the site. I accomplished this by sending out memos to all officers each week. When an officer was injured on the job, I was required to accompany the officer to the hospital. I had to complete specific paper work on each employee admitted to the hospital. I was also required to contact the director of security and the safety representative for the ISSC company. I was also required to ensure that the employees were given a drug test for each occurrence. When an employee injured themselves and did not go to the hospital, they were required to take a drug test. I interviewed each new officer that was sent to the site. I was required to ensure that all employees received the following: one security vest, one set of safety glasses, one pair of gloves, one security hat, and one gas monitor. The new employees were assigned to the post where they would be working to train for several days. They were also moved to different post to train, to enable them to become qualified to work at each post on site.

I was required to attend a safety meeting each week. The site safety representative briefed all personnel on safety violations observed during the week. They also presented pictures of safety violations that had occurred. Each attendee received safety information to use in their office and company. I performed a safety study to identify safety issues that was requested by the director of security. The site had experienced numerous accidents, and there were weekly briefings on accident prevention. The security director directed me to perform an investigation to identify causes of accidents at each post. The post on the site are listed below and the things that caused accidents:

1. Gate 1 - Stepping down from the sidewalk to the street
    - Opening and closing cabinet drawers
    - Directing vehicles entering and exiting the gate
    - Removing hot foods from the microwave oven
    - Walking on tile floors during the rainy season
2. Gate 26 - Directing traffic entering and exiting the property
    - Stepping down from the guardhouse to the street
    - Opening several file cabinet drawers at the same time

3. Scales - Walking on wet floors during rainy season
   - Stepping down from the building to the street
4. Turnstiles - Walking on wet floors during the rainy season
   - Opening and closing entry doors
5. Gate 23 - Directing vehicles entering and exiting the site
   - Walking down the steps from the building
   - Opening and closing the gate exiting the property
   - Walking on wet floors in the guardhouse
6. Muffin Property - Walking up and down the steps to the guardhouse
   - Walking on slippery floors during rainy season
   - Opening can food without proper utensils
7. Gate 43 - Walking down and up the steps to the guardhouse
   - Walking on slippery floors during rainy season
   - Directing traffic into and off the site
   - Inspecting vehicles entering the gate
8. Tents - Opening and closing the gate to the work area
   - Removing hot food from the microwave oven
9. Gate 37 - Walking up and down steps to the guardhouse
   - Opening and closing the gate to the property
   - Directing traffic entering and exiting the area
10. Gate 15 - Walking up and down the steps to the guardhouse
    - Walking on slippery floors in the guardhouse
    - Removing hot food from the microwave oven
11. BSE - Walking up and down steps to the guardhouse
    - Walking on slippery floors in the guardhouse
    - Removing hot food from the microwave oven
12. Dock 1 - Removing hot food from the microwave oven
    - Stepping down from the guardhouse to the ground
    - Walking on wet floors

- Opening canned food for consumption
13. Dock 2 - Opening canned food for consumption
    - Removing hot food from the microwave
    - Walking on wet floors
14. Dock 3 - Opening canned food for consumption
    - Removing hot food from the microwave oven
    - Walking on wet floors during rainy seasons
15. Dock 4 - Inspecting vehicles entering the gate
    - Removing hot food from the microwave
    - Opening canned food for consumption
16. Patrol - Driving vehicles on site
    - Entering and exiting the vehicles
    - Responding to emergencies on site

After I completed the safety study, I continued to concentrate on filling the post for special requirements. When a special post was opened, I was responsible for contacting a vehicle rental company to arrange for a vehicle. Sometimes I had several rental vehicles on site during the same time period. I knew the manager of the rental company, and on several occasions I could not pick up the vehicles. The manager of the rental company directed his employees to drive the vehicles to the site. The officers on the site could not use their personal vehicles on the post. I was also responsible for ensuring that the security vehicles assigned to the site were serviced. I set up an account with a local service company to monitor and repair the security vehicles. The human resource office personnel would send an employee listing, showing names of employees required to take the drug test. The drug test was required to be taken by the employees in a required amount of time.

On several occasions the employees delayed reporting to take the drug test or did not take the test. Those employees were terminated from the company. I also had to ensure that each employee had the proper uniforms. The uniforms had to be maintained in good working condition. When the employees experienced pay problems, I informed them to bring in a copy of their pay stub. After I researched the pay problem, I contacted the payroll representative, and the problems were resolved. I maintained a copy of the pay sheets in the office to review when an employee stated that their pay was incorrect. The officers continued to have accidents, and the security company was placed on probation. The client representative met with the security team president and vice president. He discussed preventive measures to use to prevent and reduce accidents.

I continued to work from 6:00 am. to 6:00 p.m. Mondays through Fridays. My manager came to the office one day and stated that I was working too much overtime, and I must change my hours. I changed my schedule to 6:00 a.m. to 2:00 p.m. I continued to manage the account and took preventive measures to reduce accidents. The last accident that I managed occurred when an employee was patrolling and fell on her knee. The correct procedures were followed to manage the accidents. When the accident occurred, I was informed by the safety manger that the employee was required to take a drug test. I contacted the employee and informed her to come to the site to take the drug test.

When she arrived on site, I met her in the parking lot and drove her to the office to take the drug test. Several days later I was informed by my manager that I did not manage the accident correctly. Several days later my manager arrived at the site, and he informed me that I was being removed from the account. I left the site and contacted the human resource representative the following day. I informed the representative that I was filing a wrongful termination request against the company. I also filed for unemployment. The unemployment official contacted me the following day and asked me questions about my termination. I received several unemployment checks before returning to work.

I was home for several weeks before the human resources representative contacted me and stated that there was a post available if I wanted it. On Monday morning I reported to the new site and began to train as a gate officer. I remained at the post for two weeks and decided that the post was not for me. I contacted the human resources office representative and informed them that I did not want to work at the gate post. Several weeks later, I was contacted by the human resource office representative and informed to go to the Westlake Park site, and interview with the site manager for a shift supervisor opening.

After the interview, the site manager informed me that I would be working from 10:00 p.m. to 6:00 a.m. five days per week. My job description reads as follows:

> Plans, supervises and coordinates security shift operations. Leads and participates in the provisions of security services such as monitoring, training and assessing the performance of security officers. Assists in the training of security personnel. Monitors the performance of security employees. Develops work schedules and make shift assignments. Monitors contracted security services operation. Conducts investigations and writes reports regarding complaints of theft and vandalism. Responds to all emergencies and provide assistance. Assists the security manager as needed. Assists the manager with interviews of new applicants. Counsels and write up employees when required. Recommends employees when required.

After working several weeks training with a supervisor from 10: 00 p.m. to 6:00 a.m., I was transferred to the day shift. The day shift was Mondays through Fridays 6:00 a.m. to 2:00 p.m., and the supervisor in the position was leaving. I began training with the supervisor for several days before he left the site. There are two different security companies on the site. The company that I am employed with have officers working in two buildings on the site. The clients are very demanding, and the officers are constantly being monitored. I visited each officer on their post each day to perform a uniform inspection. During the inspection I check for the following:

Officers have up to the minute daily activity reports uniform compliance

1. All officers have signed in for their shift.
2. The officers are not using their cell phones.
3. Check the fire panel and FCR for neatness.
4. Check the key inventory books for both signatures of the outgoing and incoming officer.

5. Ensure that each console have charged flashlights.
6. Ensure that the AED, oxygen tank, captivate screens, bullhorns, and defibrillator are working.

There are three shifts on the site. Some officers work the first shift from 6:00 a.m. to 2:00 p.m. The other officers work the 2:00 p.m. to 10:00 p.m. and 10:00 p.m. to 6:00 a.m. shifts. Some of the post are manned seven days per week. I was content on the night shift, but I am happy working on the day shift. The schedule for the upcoming week is completed on Thursdays of each week. My manager trained me to schedule the officers that only work thirty-six hours per week, to work overtime before the other officers are scheduled. This strategy keeps the overtime hours down to a minimum. When there are call-offs and officers report to duty late, I write them up, and points are assessed against them. Sometimes when officers wanted to be off, I inform them to switch shifts because there will not be any overtime hours. When there is an officer at other sites with less than forty hours and we have an opening, they work at our site. Each site is responsible for maintaining their overtime at a certain percentage.

There are certain reports that must be generated and forwarded to the main office each month. The reports must be accurate because the clients are charged based on the information received. We train officers that come from other sites to work at our site. The manager trained me how to put the reports together. I do not know how long I will continue to work as a security officer. I am now sixty-three years old. I will be eligible to draw social security in a few years. If I had elected to draw social security at sixty-two years old, I would only receive $1,100 per month. I cannot afford to take care of my family on that amount of money. I will continue to work until I am sixty-six years old because I will receive more money, and I can work and earn as much money as I desire to earn. If I had elected to draw social security at sixty-two, I could only earn $14,000 per year. This amount would be that amount that I would be stuck with receiving forever. The only way the social security process can be changed is through Congress.

There are numerous senior citizens that cannot afford to purchase medicine and pay their rent. I can pay my rent, and I get my medicine through the military hospital. I have written to some senators about the social security issue. I have not received a reply from the senators at this time.

I am responsible for responding to all emergencies in both buildings. Listed below are two emergency codes and elevator-entrapment procedures that are listed to implement during the emergencies:

1. Code blue - Medical emergencies
    -   Call 911 and give building information.
    -   Make East Lake All Call.
    -   Send the first officer that reports to the elevator with the keys to lock off the elevator. The medical bag is carried to the area where the victim is located.

2. Code Orange
    a. Fire Alarm
        -   Acknowledge the alarm
        -   Make East Lake All Call and give location.
        -   Make the building floor announcement.
        -   Call 911 with location.
        -   Get out the fireman's box key and elevator keys (give to the rover).

    a. Elevator entrapment
        -   Answer the call and note the floor and cab number.
        -   Attempt to recall the elevator to the first floor.
        -   During business hours make the East Lake All Call..
        -   After business hours contact your supervisor.
        -   Call the elevator company and get an ETA Inform the manager and passenger of the ETA
        -   During certain times the buildings must be placed in test when work is being performed.
        -   When a request is made to place the building in test, the engineers and property manager must be contacted. The name of the person making the request, authorized engineer and the duration that the company will be

performing the work. The officer will make the call to place the building in test.

When the call is made I give my name, pass code, and address, and the time the building need to be in test. Power outages before 5:00 p.m. make East Lake All Call: "Attention all units, we have a power outage. Go to the FCR room and use the phone next to the fire panel and make the announcement." After 5:00 p.m., contact the engineers and supervisors at East Lake 5 to notify them. Make announcement over PA system. Send the rover to the central plan to check alarms and elevators during the power outages. I along with the other security officers must prevent employees from Entering the elevators. The elevators change to emergency power when there is a power outage.

There are only two elevators that can be used when there is a power outage. The employees will become entrapped if they attempt to use the other elevators. This is my duties as a shift manager: immediate response to all emergency situations takes precedence over all other responsibilities. The amount of time required for the successful completion of these is "over and above" routine duties. These emergencies include medical, fire alarms. Bomb threats, suspicious persons, violence in the workplace, natural disasters, and hostile intrusions. As such the shift manager evaluates the situation, directs security control to summon all necessary resources to handle the emergency, maintains emergency communications, and makes the necessary callouts to notify all necessary authorities of the status of the event.

If necessary, the shift manager performs or directs other security officers to perform appropriate first aid procedures, including CPR to stabilize the victims. After termination of the emergency, the shift manager documents all details of the incident. The amount of time spent in performing these duties varies week to week depending on the circumstances and clients' needs. The shift's manager's responsibilities include but are not limited to the following duties:

1. Review and review written pass downs from outgoing shift managers

2. Discuss current security status with outgoing shift managers.

3. Ensure that all officers are on duty At their required posts.

4. Contact officers for coverage for all officers absent or late for duty.

5. Ensure that radio checks are made with each officer when they report on duty.

6. Ensure dissemination of access requirements to appropriate posts.

7. Review barred photos of Individuals not allowed on site.

8. Ensure confidential preparation and dissemination of New barred listings.

9. Place officers on standby to cover special coverage's that arise.

10. Perform post checks on each shift to check officers for appearance and performance.

11. Conduct on the job training for all newly assigned officers and on updated material.

12. Review daily activity reports and how to write the reports.

13. Train the officers on how to write the incident reports.

14. Coordinate training schedules with the project manager.

15. Review customer request for extended coverage and or termination of coverage.

16. Perform disciplinary counseling as required.

17. Review post orders and general orders.

18. Order supplies for each post to function properly.

19. Review incoming correspondence and ensure proper dissemination is made.

20. Participate in shift manager's meetings.

21. Prepare evaluations for officers as required.

We have the first African American president in office. Banks and other financial institutions were in financial trouble, and they requested help from the federal government. Americans have lost jobs all over the country because the United States went into a recession. Billions of dollars are being spent to fund the wars. The American people expect the president to end the war, create jobs for the unemployed, and bring the country out of the recession. Some of the financial problems occurred because of top managers and CEOs. Some of them have been placed in jail for their crimes.

When the automobile companies, closed numerous employees lost their jobs The federal government had to and continues to approve funds to be allocated to states for those that are unemployed. During the election year, more people from different nationalities came out to vote than ever before. Some of the people that did not vote informed me that their vote did not matter. Some people informed me that their vote would not change anything. I informed them that all votes counted and were important and made a difference. My grandfather and father were Democrats when they were alive. This is one reason I am a Democrat, and I believe in what the party stands for. When Barack Obama was elected, my wife and I watched the vote count on election night until the last vote came in for each state. When President Obama made the speech that he was running for president, I was reminded of the speech that John F. Kennedy made. The speeches were similar to me. The younger adults and women came out to vote and ensured that Barack Obama was elected to president. History was made when President Obama became the first African American president.

My wife and I are part of the history. We want our grandchildren and their children to one day say my grandparents made history, when they voted to help elect the first African American to become president of the United States. We do not have many minority representatives in the Senate and Congress. More minorities will be encouraged to run for office after realizing what is possible in the United States.

I have decided to write a second book. I realize from being raised on a farm and my family being farmers that, I wanted to obtain an education that would enable me to seek a different line of employment. I also realize now that the farmers must be supported because they are people that feed the country. I do not agree with the government when a limit on the amount of food a farmer can produce is enforced. We are forced to pay more for some foods because the food is grown in other countries. Numerous minority kids and adults realized that they could accomplish anything they desired. I have been encouraged to complete writing this book and plan to pursue a PhD. People all over the world were elated when Barack Obama won the presidential election.

I continue to be employed in the security industry, and it has not been affected by the recession. The security industry is hiring more employees because there is a great demand. Employees that work at the same company as I remain employed, if they report to work on time and perform their job. They also must present a professional appearance when reporting for their shift. I inspect all the officers on my shift each day to ensure they are in compliance. When they report late for their shift, I write them up. I must maintain my standards above the average to set an example for the other officers. I normally arrive at the site thirty minutes before my shift begins. This gives me ample time to receive a briefing from the supervisor that I relieved from duty.

I was at the store one day and decided to purchase a tomato for use on hamburgers. The cost was almost three dollars for the tomato, and I decided that we could survive without that tomato. The working-class people are forced to pay the high cost for foods. The cost of foods does not matter to the rich people because they can afford to pay the prices. Our pay must be increased, and the cost to live must be reduced to give the working-class and poor people a chance in life. The poor people suffer more than the nonpoor because many of them were just surviving prior to the rise in prices. There are many children that do not have a chance in schools because they leave home hungry. I have and continue to encourage my family members to pursue an education to give them a chance at getting the good job. I have not received that good job at this point in life, but I am continuing to try to improve my life. I am also preparing a future for my family so they will not be forced to take the low-paying jobs. Presently I have an individual retirement account that I put money into.

I am writing this book that I hope will be a best seller and generate millions in sales. I plan to generate fifty thousand dollars to place in a high-interest account. I have developed a barbecue sauce that I will have placed in grocery stores. I have developed a new pizza that I plan to get produced and into stores. My IRA will be converted into a CD. Once income begins to be generated from each source, certain percentages will be invested. Numerous people are using coupons when shopping for food due to the recession. I remove coupons from the Sunday newspaper when my wife is too busy. I also use coupons for oil changes for the vehicles. The cost for the oil change without the coupons makes the price to be $25 to $30. When we have birthday parties for the employees at work, I use the coupons to pick up items to carry to the party. My family is able to save money when we purchase certain items from the store. We have to ensure that we use the coupons before they expire.

Eight years ago my wife was backing her vehicle from the drive-way at our home, when another driver drove his vehicle into her vehicle. She only had several payments left to make on her vehicle before it was paid off. When the accident was reported to the insurance company, they totaled the vehicle. My wife was forced to search for another vehicle because she required transportation to work. During her search she located a 2003 Hyundai Accent. The vehicle was test-driven, and my wife decided that she wanted to purchase the vehicle. The vehicle was financed for three years, and full-coverage insurance had to be purchased. I also was driving a vehicle that was being financed. We have decided not to have two vehicles financed at the same time. We have decided not to have vehicle payments for five to ten years.

I plan to purchase a home in the future because I want something to pass down to our children. We are presently renting a home in Stafford, Texas. We realize that a large down payment must be made on the home to have comfortable payments. I have worked for fortune 100 and 500 companies for fourteen years. The oil companies that I am presently working at continues to hire new employees. The companies hire more people from other countries than African Americans. Some people from foreign countries cannot speak English that can be understood. I went online attempting to get a count for the number of African Americans that are employed at the companies. I could not get a correct number for my request. I think the company managers do not want to hire African Americans, especially males. Some African American females are hired, but more female Caucasians are hired than any other nationality. If this practice continues, the high-paying jobs will continue to be held by the Caucasians. I can count the number of African American males that are employed at the company on one hand. One of the companies employs approximately four to five hundred employees. I have not seen many African American males come to the companies for an interview. I think this is a form of discrimination being used to keep the African American out of the workforce. The African American male cannot survive unless he is employed. I think the federal government must begin to investigate the hiring practices of those companies.

One day I asked why there were such a small number of African Americans employed at the companies. I was informed that they did not know about the job requirements. I also stated that I know there have to be some qualified African Americans graduating from college that can work at the companies. The affirmative action used in the past must be used now to ensure everyone is given a fair shake.

On March 2010, our daughter Gloria Barker gave birth to our fifteenth grandchild. His name is Christian Taylor Barker. My wife and I love him very much. Normally when I arrive from work, I have a chance to hold him and talk with him. My wife takes care of him when our daughter is working. When he was born, he wanted to eat every two hours. I was given the task of warming his bottle and giving it to my wife to feed him. When the time comes, I want him to attend the best schools and graduate. Next, I want him to go to college and become a lawyer or doctor and have a successful life. We have fourteen other grandchildren who are older than Christian.

My life up to this point has been good. I had some of the best parents anyone could have. They were not rich, but they worked hard to provide for our family. My father never complained about going to work in rain, snow, or heat. My parents did not earn much money during those times, but we survived. Some of the same things that I have done in life I would do the same things again if I had to repeat my life over again. I would enter the military and travel over the world. If I had not entered the military, I would not have met my wife. We have been together for thirty-nine years and look for many more. We have five children and fifteen grandchildren and eleven great-grandchildren. The only part of my life that I would change are the employers that I worked for. I would not waste all those years working in the security industry because I cannot retire from this industry. I have worked for other companies on a temporary basis. I have other avenues I plan to explore such as becoming a senator or congressman. I plan to own my business and develop a system to train minority children in science and math.

WHAT LIFE MEANS TO ME

Life to me means having a family that is healthy and prosperous. I am happy most of my life. I don't understand why life is so difficult for my people. We just want to accomplish certain things in life such as a good education, good job, a healthy family that serve God. For some reason, we have the highest high school dropout rate in the United States. Today our nation faces a dropout crisis. One cause of the high dropout rate is due to the authority to spank our children. The parents cannot discipline the children properly unless they spank them. Some of the young adults have decided to drop out of school because they feel they are adults and should be able to choose their path in life. The kids that decide to drop out of school are determining their future. The kids that drop out of school limit their job potential in the future. They will only be able to get the low paying jobs.

When I was growing up my parents always encouraged me to complete high school to make myself more marketable for employment. I obtained education levels far beyond the high school level. I used the same procedure with our children by encouraging them to complete high school and college.

A world where illegal drugs does not exist. A world where Americans will not have to depend on other countries for oil support. A world that provides free health care for all Americans. A system that forces kids to stay in school until they graduate. A world where teenage pregnancy does not exist. A system where healthy males cannot receive SSI checks from the government. A system where more African Americans graduate from high school, college, and the number is more than there are in jails. A cure for the AIDS virus. A system where the color of a person's skin color does not have an effect on the type job he is hired to fill. A judicial system where African Americans are not given more jail time than someone from another nationality for the same crime. A country where four ten-hour work days are the normal work week. A system where more vehicles are made in America and less purchased from other countries. A system where more jobs are kept in the United States and less transferred to other countries. A system that limits the number of people that can become American citizens each year. A system that will not allow foreign people to enter into the United States with criminal records. A system where drunk drivers that cause lives to end lose their driver's license forever. A system where the internal revenue cannot charge interest for taxes owed. A system that will permit a person sixty-two years of age that receives social security to work as much as they desire without affecting their check. A system that reduces the food prices for all senior citizens. A system that provides free food to all senior citizens that cannot afford to purchase the food. A system that ensures that all people who have worked all their lives receives the required amount of money to survive on. A system that pays for all seniors medical and prescription drugs. A cure for all major diseases. A judicial system that have the same laws for all people. A world that all people live in peace and do not have wars anywhere in the world. The security career is not the career that I planned to pursue when I retired from the air force.

I have used the security career field to add to my retirement pay and live and take care of my family. This is a job that the pay is low, and the job expectations are high. Many of the clients do not appreciate the security officers until something happens, and they are needed. I have worked at different companies throughout the industry. If I was not receiving a monthly retirement check, I would not be able to pay my bills. I am employed by a security company that provides security for several oil companies. The companies employ numerous foreign workers and very few African Americans. I think the good old boy syndrome is still working in the oil industry hiring process. The oil company's buildings have more Caucasian females employed than any other nationality. I think the oil company's management has one thing in mind, keep the minority people in the low income jobs and to only hire them for the none management jobs. The government should take control of the gas price increases. Private and corporate gas station owners should be directed by the government when and how often gas prices can be increased.

The gas prices have dropped to $3.65 per gallon, and I can fill my gas tank without almost spending $100.00. We have a family trip planned for the summer and we will be driving for approximately eight to ten hours. I will be required to fill the gas tank several times during the trip. Today the gas price per gallon is $3.49, and I filled my tank for $57.00. I have obtained my educational degrees to ensure that I obtain a good-paying job. I have an associate of arts, bachelor of science, and a master of arts degree. I have also been accepted into a PhD program. I have not been successful in obtaining that good-paying job that I can retire from. I am now sixty-three years old, and age is working against me in obtaining that good job that I can retire from. I am continuing to search for a good-paying job that will give me another retirement check, to go with my military check and social security when I receive it. I have an individual retirement account that I place money into. I am planning to open a market money account and purchase stocks and bonds. I also have a new pizza and sauce that I plan to place on the market. I have always wanted to work for the federal government in some capacity. If this happens, I will only work long enough to become eligible for retirement. I am sending out résumés and searching on the Internet for other employment.

We will relocate to Sacramento, California, within the next six months. I have been making vehicle payments for the majority of my adult life. When the SUV is paid off, I will be free of vehicle payments. I plan to have a good five to ten years where I can live free of vehicle payments. The money being paid for my vehicle will be placed in a high interest bearing account such as an annuity. The vehicle payment for my SUV is $385 per month. The vehicle that I am making payments on is a 2005 Mercury Mountaineer. I recently paid for transmission work and a tune-up. I have also purchased four new tires and replaced the brake shoes. I also plan to replace all the belts, hoses, and struts. The struts for the front will cost $475, which include labor. The vehicle should last for a long time after all the parts have been replaced. I have paid off my wife's vehicle and I only have to keep it tuned, oil changed, and the wheels aligned. The vehicle should last for a long time before we are forced to search for another vehicle.

When we relocate to Sacramento, California, we will rent or lease a house when we arrive. I plan to purchase a home in the near future because it makes good sense to purchase. I do not plan to continue to pay someone's mortgage for them. If we continue to rent, that is what we will be doing. My wife is tired of working in the job she has been doing. I plan to have everything set up where she does not have to work unless she wants to. She will probably assist in the care of my grandson; we will drop him at day care and pick him up from day care.

We went to Fairfield,. California, in June 2012 for our great-grandson's high school graduation. We flew from Hobby airport in Houston, Texas, to Oakland, California. We picked up a rental vehicle and drove to Sacramento, California, and stayed with our daughter Gloria, grandson Christian, and son-in-law Derrick. We arose each morning and ate breakfast, and on Friday we all went to the crab shack. On Saturday morning we drove to Fairfield, California, to our granddaughter Makita and Ernest's home. They are the parents of our great-grandsons.

The graduation was held at ten o'clock on Saturday morning at Fairfield High School Stadium. After the graduation we returned to Makita and Ernest's home for a graduation celebration at 3:00 p.m. There were approximately fifty to sixty family members and friends at the celebration. Some of the family members played basketball, shot pool, and watched the NBA playoffs. When we left, we visited some old friends that lived in Fairfield, California. The following day we visited some friends that lives in Vacaville, California.

Mr. Curl and I were stationed together in the military at Travis Air Force Base. I had not seen him or his family in almost twenty years. We were scheduled for our flight on Monday afternoon back to Houston, Texas. Our daughter Gloria and grandson Christian were in the vehicle as we drove down the freeway to Oakland, California. Gloria looked at the plane information and discovered that we had missed our flight. Gloria called the airlines and changed our reservation to the following day. When we departed the following day, we were sad to be leaving them, and Christian was crying. We drove to the car rental and returned our vehicle and caught our flight to Houston, Texas.

I had never attended a family reunion until July 1987. My wife's family sponsored a family reunion in Blytheville Arkansas. Beulah, Gloria, Clifford, and I drove from Newport News, Virginia, to Omaha, Nebraska, to meet her cousins who were also going to the reunion. When we arrived in Omaha, Beulah's cousins were ready to leave; we followed them. The drive from Omaha to Blytheville took approximately ten to thirteen hours. We all had fun driving and stopping for gas and food. Finally we arrived in Blytheville late in the afternoon. We all checked into the hotel and relaxed until it was time for the get acquainted gathering.

There was a room reserved for the gathering that we assembled in at six o'clock. There were sodas, hordes, chips, sandwiches, and fruits for the family members. When the members arrived at the hotel and checked in, they came to the get-acquainted room. The purpose of the get-acquainted gathering was to give the members a chance to meet. The gathering normally lasted for several hours. The older family members were not always known by the younger members. This gave them a chance to meet and get to know the family. The family members that had ordered T-shirts from the host received them at the gathering. The members that had not paid for the T-shirts in advance could do so at the gathering. This was my first family reunion, and I did not know my wife's family members. I only knew her parents and sisters and brothers. I had not met the family members that lived in other states.

During the get-acquainted night the members gave suggestions of things to do at the picnic on Saturday. The following day, which was Saturday, Beulah, the kids, and I drove to her parents' home. Beulah's father and I carried the ribs, chickens, hot links, and hamburgers to the park. Beulah and the kids arrived at the park later. We made a fire in two barbecue grills and waited until the fire was ready. We knew the fire was ready when the coals turned white. The meat had been washed and seasoned. We placed the ribs and chicken on the grill before the other foods because they had to cook longer. When the ribs and chicken were ready, we placed some barbecue sauce on the meat and returned it to the grill for about twenty minutes. Next, we placed the hamburgers and hot dogs on the grill to cook.

Beulah made potato salad, cakes, pies, and other condiments. Some of the other members also cooked different foods for the occasion. When the meat was ready to be removed from the grill, we removed it and placed it into the chafing dishes. We had a building that was screened in, and we used it to place the food. The chafing dishes along with the other foods were placed on six and eight-foot tables. When it was time to eat, each member picked up their plate, knife, fork, spoon, and napkin. They then proceeded down the line of tables until they had food from each pan. Water, sodas, and juices were stored in containers for consumption. Some members went through the food line one time and others several times. The food remained on the tables until the picnic ended. There were different games that members could participate in such as softball, basketball, horse shoes, volleyball, and darts. The picnic lasted all day until everyone was ready to leave.

When the picnic ended, the members returned to the hotel to relax. Some of the members entered the swimming pool, and others found different ways to relax. The members were free to do anything that they desired. Some of the members drove to Memphis, Tennessee, and some went to Jonesboro. Beulah, the kids, and I stayed in the hotel and relaxed. The following morning we ate breakfast and drove to church. After church we drove to her parents' home and spent some time with them.

Later that night a banquet was given in the hotel. Normally a buffet was set up for the dinner. We always had a program that list each thing that would occur during the night. Prizes were given to the oldest member, the youngest member, and for the member that traveled the longest distance. When dinner was completed, members that wanted to sing, dance, model, or tell jokes had the opportunity to do so. Also during the night the member that was going to host the next family reunion was announced. The addresses of the family members and any funds left over were given to the upcoming sponsor. When the banquet was over, we remained to greet and speak with the other members. When the members began to return to their rooms, we drove over to my father-in-law and mother-in-law's home. We stayed there for several hours before returning to the hotel. Beulah's brothers and sisters were always there, and we had a chance to see them and their families before we departed.

Finally we said goodbye to everyone and returned to our hotel. We turned in for the night and received a goodnight's sleep. We got up the following morning at four o'clock and began our drive to Newport, News Virginia.

In 1989, Beulah's cousins in Omaha hosted the family reunion. This was the first time that I had been to Omaha, Nebraska. We had a long drive from Virginia to Omaha. When we arrived, we stayed at Beulah's cousin's home. They showed me around the city of Omaha. We followed the same procedure for the family reunion as the previous reunion. The only difference at this family reunion was the food. The picnic and banquet was the same as the previous family reunion. This was the first time that I had met Beulah's cousins. We had a chance to visit some of the outside sources outside the family reunion. We had the get acquainted gathering on a Friday night. We cooked the food for the picnic on Saturday, and all the family members ate and enjoyed themselves. They participated in the different activities available in the park.

The banquet was held Sunday night, and all the family members attended. After the banquet the members prepared for their return home. Some of the members returned to the airport to catch their flight. Some of the members came on a chartered bus. Where there were a large number of family members that lived in the same area; they normally chartered a bus to bring them to the family reunion. My wife also had a chance to visit with her uncle and aunt that lived in Omaha, Nebraska. When there was a historic place in the city where we held the family reunion, we attempted to visit it. When the city was famous for a particular food, we visited the restaurant that sold the food. I had seen the University of Omaha football team on television for years, and I drove past the University in Omaha.

When I drove past the university, I remembered the great college and professional football players that I had watched play the game at the University of Omaha.

The following years and locations are where the family reunions were held:

1991 – Clarksdale, Mississippi	2007 – Memphis, Tennessee
1994 – Chicago, Illinois	2008 – Chicago, Illinois
1995 – St. Louis, Missouri	2009 – Fort Wayne, Indiana
1996 – Blytheville, Arkansas	2010 – Lancing, Illinois
1997 – Fort Wayne, Indiana	2011- None
1998 – Houston, Texas	2012- None
1999 – Greenville, Mississippi	2013 - Kansas City, Missouri
2000 – Chicago, Illinois	2014 – Omaha, Nebraska
2001 – Omaha, Nebraska	2015 – Blytheville, Arkansas
2005 – Chicago, Illinois	

On October 17, 2012, my wife and I celebrated thirty-nine years of marriage. The children are all adults now and some of the grand-children also. We did not plan anything special except going out to dinner to celebrate.

On the same day the ABM security company replaced the current company that I have been employed with. I along with all the other officers were required to reapply for our positions with the new company. I also had to retake a drug test and complete the same paperwork that a new employee completes. The new company also conducted a background check on me before I was guaranteed a position. The security license that I currently possess was converted over to the new company for a specific time. Everyone was not required to obtain a new security license with the new company. The cost for the license will be deducted from my pay when it is renewed. I was required to pay $250 for uniforms by having the company deduct money from my check each payday until it was paid in full. All officers were placed on a 120-day probation period. This means that during the probation period if an officer does not meet the company standards, they can be terminated from the company. The new company paid each officer for their vacation based on the date they were hired with the previous company.

The company is a larger company and offers more benefits and opportunities to advance. We must remain proficient in the emergency procedures and other job requirements. I am excited to be employed with the new company because the benefits are better.

My wife, her sister, and I drove to Blytheville, Arkansas, in November 2011 to visit her family for Thanksgiving. My wife and I awoke at 4:00 a.m. and showered, and I packed the suitcases into the vehicle. She had baked a turkey, cakes, and potato salad to carry to Arkansas. She also cooked a Turkey and dressing for our daughter Gloria and grandson Christian for Thanksgiving. I began driving on the trip, and we stopped for food and gas several times. We arrived in Arkansas at eight thirty on the night before Thanksgiving. When we arrived my sister-in-law had been sick and was not eating. We ate dinner the same night, and she began to eat. We arose on Thanksgiving Day, and my wife prepared breakfast, and she ate. When Thanksgiving dinner was served, she also ate dinner. We remained there until Sunday, and she ate each meal. She began to get stronger and was able to move around better.

We departed on Sunday morning and enjoyed a ten-hour drive to Stafford, Texas. We were happy to be back at home with our daughter and grandson. I continued to train my grandson how to ride his tricycle and play different games with him. My life up to this point has been very interesting. I would not change anything in my life but my career. I would choose a career that offer benefits and paid vacations when I am off work. I would serve the same time or longer that I served in the military. I would never have visited the countries that I went to, if I had not been in the military. I could never have afforded to pay to visit those countries. If I had to choose a country to live in outside the United States, I would choose Germany. The living conditions in Germany are similar to the conditions in the United States. The three years that I served in Germany gave me a chance to get to know some of the people and the way they lived. I had a chance to eat the food and learn about their culture. I am happy to have been given the opportunity to visit Germany.

I met my wife by visiting Oakland, California, with a friend on a Saturday. My friend introduced me to Beulah, and we dated for three years before we were married. During the years that we dated we enjoyed life and visited different malls and movies. We also went to the fair each year and took the children to different amusements. If I could change one thing in my life, I would have better credit and already have a house where Beulah and I plan to live.

I Voted for the Presidential Election

This is the year for President Barack Obama to run for reelection for president.

The state of Texas representatives are attempting to get a law passed that requires all voters to have photo identification before they are allowed to vote. This will affect African Americans and Hispanic people more than any other nationality. If this law becomes effective, the minority voters that do not have the proper identification will not be allowed to vote. The Democratic Party will be limited on the number of votes cast for the party. My ancestors died for the right to vote, and I along with my wife plan to be at the polls to vote. Numerous people are blaming President Obama for the condition of the economy. Some of them do not want to admit that the economy was in bad shape when he took office. He has done numerous things to turn the economy around. The Republicans do not agree with anything that the president does or attempts to do. I continue to encourage everyone that is eligible to vote to do so. I encourage my family members to also go to the polls to vote. In order for the president to get reelected, everyone eligible to vote must vote. He will also need some independent voters to vote for him. When I am at work during the day I ask my coworkers if they are registered to vote. If they inform me that they are not registered to vote, I inform them that they must get registered so they can vote.

There are numerous Americans that do not want to see the president reelected. The reason that they do not want to see him reelected is because he is an African American. If a person is continued to be judged based on the color of their skin, there will always be problems in the United States and the world. The people in foreign countries respect our president more than some Americans. I will be at the polls along with my wife to vote for the reelection of President Barack Obama. I wrote the president a letter suggesting that he stop bashing Mitt Romney and concentrate on the economy. I informed him that he must start campaigning on how to create jobs. I also suggested that he should inform the American people what his plans are for the future. He also should inform the American people what he plans to do to help them in the future. He must work on creating jobs by holding each state responsible. The jobs should come from rebuilding bridges, railroads, schools, and freeways.

My wife and I have been discussing our upcoming move back to Sacramento, California. We are deciding on the type of residence we should live in. I may not be employed when we arrive there so we must have a residence that we can afford to pay for each month. I have been going on the Internet several times per week searching for employment. I do not plan to go back into the security industry, but I may be forced to, if I do not have another type job. I am also considering teaching at the university online. When we arrive in California, I must be employed, because I cannot afford to be without a job for a long period of time. We will have my military retirement and Beulah's social security to live on in the beginning. I am not going to draw my social security until I become sixty-six years old. I can draw the social security now, but I will only receive $1,398 per month. If I wait, the social security check will be substantially more. Also I will be able to work as much as possible once I become sixty-six years old. Presently if I receive social security, I will only be permitted to work part-time. My life insurance payments will also increase as I become older. I also plan to have funds coming in from other sources such as my books, barbecue pizza sauce, pizza, and 401(k) plan. I plan to have only the essential bills that is required to survive. I feel that I have a good plan for the future and life will be good for Beulah and I.

LETTER TO MY FAVORITE AUNT

Aunt Lillie Mae Hairston was our father's youngest sister in the Hodge family. She had been married to Obie Jack Hairston for years before he passed away. After uncle Jack passed away, she could not live alone. She was placed in a convalescent home. I would call her on the phone occasionally while she could hear. After she lost her hearing, I began to write her every other week. When I began to write her, I sent the letters to my first cousin Shirley Wooten. Later I sent her letters to my other first cousin Carolyn S. Brown, and she read the letters to her and kept me informed about her health. Aunt Lillie Mae eventually developed pneumonia and was placed in the hospital. She had a birthday in August 2012 and she celebrated her eighty-ninth birthday. The last letter that I wrote to her was dated August 19, 2012. Carolyn called on August 20, 2012, and stated That she received a call from the hospital at 3:00 a.m. that Aunt Lillie Mae had passed away in her sleep. I had not mailed the last letter that I had written to her. When I spoke with Carolyn, I informed her about the letter. I mailed the letter to Carolyn, and I know Aunt Lillie Mae will look down from heaven and read my last letter that I wrote her. I will miss you, Aunt Lillie Mae.

Mr. President, I am sitting here in the hospital waiting room on a Saturday afternoon. My wife had a procedure, and I am waiting for her recovery. I decided to write you with some suggestions to help reduce the federal debt and stimulate the economy. The military troops have been removed from Iraq, and this is good. The American government must not rebuild Iraq. We cannot afford to rebuild their economy. The Iraq people are adjusted to living their way of life, and we do not need to try to change it. The people do not want Americans there, so you should remove all the military immediately. The American government is spending millions of dollars each day to fund the war in Afghanistan that we cannot afford to spend. American soldiers are losing their lives and receiving permanent injuries that cannot be repaired. Lost legs, arms, and eyes are not replaceable. The artificial arms and legs are not the same as the original. Some injured soldiers never become adjusted to the artificial limbs. You must bring all the military troops home today. The families that lost loved ones, they never completely recover from the lost. The Afghanistan people do not want Americans there. The Russians could not win there, and we cannot win.

The Afghanistan government must take the lead in the fight against terrorism. The money being used to fund the war can be used to reduce the debt and hire more teachers, policemen, doctors, lawyers, scientists, and engineers. We must not rebuild the Afghanistan economy because their economy would be in bad shape if we were not there. More jobs must be created to reduce the unemployment and remove people from the food stamp program. There are 46.7 million people receiving food stamps. Some of the people must be removed from the program, such as single healthy men that are not searching for employment. While they are receiving food stamps, they must continue to search for employment each day. They must turn in a weekly list of employers that have job openings they applied for. The single females that have children must also search for employment. The same rules apply to them as the males. When they began the program with two children, this must be the limit that they receive food stamps for. If they decide to have additional children, they must not be given food stamps.

The day care for children is expensive and almost out of reach for the mothers. When a mother or single male receives $800 in food stamps and get a job earning $700 for a two-week period, $400 must be used toward the purchase of the food stamps. The food stamp program is out of control and is not being managed as it should be. The federal government must make the state governments responsible for managing the program. Each person that is receiving food stamps must be rescreened to determine if they are eligible for the program. Once their eligibility is determined they should receive the food stamps based on each case.

There must be a limit placed on the number of foreigners entering the United States each year to become citizens of the United States. We have a high unemployment rate and cannot afford to allow people to enter from other countries that the government are forced to provide support for. The people that are applying for entry should not be allowed to enter unless they are educated with a skill that is needed. We need doctors, lawyers, dentist, nurses, teachers, and some other hard-to-fill professional posts. These people must be able to be employable in the United States. When they arrive they must be required to have a specific amount of funds to live on until they become employed. When a doctor and his wife and children are permitted to enter the United States, this should not mean that his brothers, sisters, aunts, uncles, and cousins are also allowed to enter. People with criminal records should not be permitted to enter the United States. The unemployment rate will not go down as long as people from all over the world are allowed to enter the United States. The American government must decline to permit people to enter the United States from countries with terrorist. The people coming from the Middle East must be monitored when entering the United States. We do not know who we are permitting to enter. Presently the demonstrations are in other countries; we do not want the violence to come to our country. The people coming from Mexico to work on the farms and in other areas should be allowed to enter if the employers obtain identification cards for each individual. The funds these workers earn must be taxed by the American government. When an individual becomes sixty-two years old and decides to apply for social security, he/she can earn only $14,000 per year. This means the individuals can only work part-time. I do not believe anyone can survive if they only work part-time. If the individuals are working part-time, less money is going into the social security fund.

I think all individuals should be allowed to work as much as possible at age sixty-two and receive their social security without a penalty. The more an individual work, the more money will go into the social security fund. This is a law that must be changed by Congress to allow individuals to work as much as possible at age sixty-two and receive social security. The Medicare program is out of control and must be managed to eliminate the money that is being lost by the government. Each governor in each state must be held responsible for the programs in their state. Funds must not be approved for the program without positive proof of service. This will eliminate funds from being paid for service that is not received. I think someone should be appointed in each city and county to monitor the program in their area. The size of the federal government must be reduced. Employees that have been employed for a specific number of years and are sixty-two and older should be offered a retirement package.

Employees that are fifty-five years old should also be offered a package based on the number of years they have been employed. The federal government must place a freeze on hiring for five years. The civil service positions must be changed from a forty-hour workweek to a thirty-two-hour workweek. Some government task must also be contracted out to other companies. Institute a 90 percent reduction in the federal government's annual travel budget. Require a 20 percent reduction in the size of the federal work force and in the federal contracted workforce. The current freeze must be extended for five years. All bonuses, including performance and recruitment, should be frozen. Cut defense spending to 50 percent. Close some military bases in other countries and bring the military personnel home. The government vehicles used to transport federal workers must be discontinued.

Today is October 4, 2013, and I am sixty-five years young. I thank God for blessing me to see another birthday. I plan to live a long prosperous life. We planned to go out for dinner to celebrate my birthday but my wife had surgery on October 3, and we had to cancel. I normally do not request that I be given many things for my birthday. This year I informed my wife to purchase a shirt and tie for my birthday. I informed our daughter Gloria and grandson Christian to send a birthday card. Some of the other children normally call and wish me a happy birthday. I plan to begin my walking program and lose weight. My blood pressure has been high for several weeks, and I am working on lowering it to a reasonable level. When I am in the store to purchase food, I always check the sodium content before I make a purchase. When I purchase foods with sodium, I ensure that the sodium content is low or does not contain any sodium.

My wife had surgery on October 3, 2012, and I had to take off from work to drive her to the hospital. We also had to cancel our dinner plans because I had to work to make up for the time that I took off for her surgery. I informed my wife that we could pick up some food and bring it home after the birthday. We decided to pick up some chicken, red beans, and rice. I plan to eat more healthy foods and do the things to keep my body more healthy. I checked the Internet for a list of foods that assist in lowering my blood pressure and blood sugar.

In 1965, I was a sophomore in high school and I was not old enough to vote in the state or federal elections. I was aware of the different tactics used to prevent my people from voting. Prior to the passage of the Voting Rights Act of 1965, my people could not vote.

> The act was passed in response to Jim Crow laws and other restrictions on minorities voting rights at the time. The murder of voting rights activists in Philadelphia Mississippi gained national attention, along with numerous other acts of violence and terrorism. There was an unprovoked attack on March 7, 1965 by state Troopers on peaceful marchers crossing the Edmund Pettis bridge in Selma Alabama in route to the state capital in Montgomery, persuaded President Johnson and Congress to overcome southern legislators registance to effective voting rights legislation. President Johnson

signed the legist ion into law on August 6, 1965. (http//
civil-rights.findlaw.com/otherconstitutional-rig.)

I informed my parents and friends that I would always vote when there
is an election. I vote because my people suffered and lost their lives so my
people, and I can have the right to vote. Voting is my right and I owe it
to myself to vote in every election that I choose. I am shocked the ways
some people that do not vote and do not see the importance of voting. I
will always vote in the presidential elections and some state elections. Early
voting for president of the United States began on October 22, 2012. My
wife and I voted early because we did not want to fight the long line of voters
on November 6, 2012. We made history for a second time in our lives, by
voting for the reelection of President Barak Obama to become president of
the United States. When we voted at previous polls, the workers asked for our
driver's license and scanned the license on the computer. When we arrived at
the polls this time we presented our voter registration cards, and did not have
to present our license. Different things are being used to discourage voters
from voting. Some states require voters to have a photo identification card
before they are permitted to vote. Numerous senior citizens and minorities
do not have photo identification cards or transportation to get to the polls. I
continue to encourage my family, friends, and coworkers to go to the poles
and vote early. My wife and I have a driver's license, military identification
card, and a voter registration card.

Once my wife and I voted we were issued a sticker that had "I voted"
on the sticker. I placed the sticker on the outside of my work blazer and
returned to work. My coworkers noticed the sticker on my blazer and asked
if I had voted. Some of my coworkers remembered to vote early when they
noticed the sticker on my coat. I reminded some of the younger coworkers
that were voting for the first time, to ensure that they were registered before
attempting to vote. One of my coworkers had moved after the last election,
and I asked if he put in a change of address. He stated that he had put in a
change of address and should be able to vote.

I contacted my brother in Virginia and reminded him to vote. I also
called my daughter in California to remind her about voting. I received a
jury summons a week before I went to the polls to vote. When I reported
for jury duty, I was the seventh person on the front row in the courtroom.
Six jurors were selected to hear the case, and I was not selected. I did not feel

discouraged for not being selected because I would have gladly served on the jury.

My wife and I celebrated our thirty-ninth wedding anniversary on October 17, 2012. We had a special dinner planned. We went to the new steak restaurant and both of us ordered steaks for dinner. I always inform Beulah that I have been married to her longer than I was single. She always tell me that I have enjoyed the best part of her life. We have traveled over the United States making military moves from state to state. I have gone to different countries, leaving the family in the states when they could not accompany me. I remember a house where we lived that did not have a patio. Beulah informed me that she wanted a patio so she could sit outside. I measured an area of the yard off to the specific requirement. Once the area was measured off, I dug the area out and leveled it. I contacted a cement company and gave the associate the patio size. I was given the amount of cement required for the area and the cost. The delivery date was scheduled on a Saturday, and the truck arrived with the cement. The cement truck driver drove to the curve of our home. I pushed a wheelbarrow to the curve, and the truck driver filled it with cement. I rolled the wheelbarrow to the patio area and dumped the cement. My friend spread and leveled the cement each time that I dumped it.

When I completed dumping, the cement I assisted my friend with spreading it. We left the cement to set and dry for one to two weeks. Once the cement was dry, my wife informed me that she wanted a cover over the patio so she could sit outside and not be exposed to the sun. I purchased several posts and dug several holes and placed each in a separate hole with cement around each. Once the posts were stable and the cement became hard, I purchased wood for the top and constructed a top. During the rainy season water leaked onto the patio, and I purchased some tar and roofing to repair the leaks. My wife was right next to me during the construction of the patio top.

Today is January 25, 2013, and I am working the night shift from 10:00 p.m. to 6:00 a.m. the next day. One of my coworkers was sick and could not work. I am very happy today because my blood pressure is lower than it has been in years. Listed below are readings during some days in December 2012 and January 2013:

December 30 2012 155/83	January 20, 2013, 136/73
December 31 2012, 169/94	January 22, 2013, 140/80
January 1, 2013, 168/89	January 24, 2013, 142/76
January 6 2013, 159/84	January 25, 2013, 139/75
January 7, 2013, 156/79	January 26, 2013, 142/81
January 10, 2013, 153/78	January 27, 2013, 124/67
January 12, 2013, 160/80	January 28, 2013, 139/68
January 15, 2013, 170/85	January 29, 2013, 128/68
January 16, 2013, 163/86	January 30, 2013, 141/70
January 17, 2013, 143/76	January 31, 2013, 140/71

I requested that my family practice doctor change the blood pressure medicine I was taking because it was not working. I began to eat foods and vegetables that help reduce high blood pressure. When I visit the store to purchase food, the first thing I check for is the sodium content. The medicine that the doctors prescribe cannot always do the job alone. There must be something to give assistance. I stay away from foods that are high in sodium. I love bologna, and I have made sandwiches for years and sometimes ate it right out of the refrigerator. Several years ago my doctor informed me to stop eating bologna, and I stopped. There are numerous soul foods that I love to eat. I realize that I cannot eat those foods anymore if I want to maintain a low blood pressure. These are foods that I grew up eating as a child. When I was growing up as a child I did not have a choice of the type food to eat. Today I control my own destiny when deciding the different type foods to eat. My wife and I also eat more grilled and baked foods and less fried foods.

Today is the day before the Super Bowl, and I decided to purchase a few snacks. When I entered the store, the first thing I did was check the sodium content on the food, before making a purchase. I plan to live a long healthy life by eating the right foods and the proper diet and exercise.

Our great-grandson Evan V. Wright graduated from Fairfield high school in Fairfield California on June 7, 2013. We were unable to attend the graduation ceremony, but we sent Evan a good graduation present. Evan is the second of three sons in his family to graduate from high school. I remember when Evan's mother, Makita Lucas, our granddaughter, was raising Evan and his brothers. Erik, his older brother, graduated a year before he graduated. I think Evan plans to enter the United States Air Force. Makita have always encouraged Evan to complete high school. Evan realizes that completing high school is an important step to accomplishing his life goals. We visited Evan and his family a week later to personally congratulate him on his graduation from high school.

On June 16, 2013, my wife Beulah and I flew to Oakland California and rented a vehicle to attend our grandson Nathan E. McAllister's high school graduation. After landing in Oakland, we drove to Sacramento, California, and stayed with our daughter Gloria Barker, Christian, and Derek Barker. On Friday night we went to old Sacramento for dinner. Our grandson Tarvio McAllister treated us to dinner.

On Saturday morning we arose early and departed from Sacramento, California at 6:00 a.m. for Union City, California. We arrived at James Logan High School at 8:00 a.m. to attend the commencement exercise. The parking lot at the school was full with vehicles when we arrived. Most of the people had to drive around in the parking lot and attempt to find a parking space or park on the street. The ceremony began at 8:30 a.m. and lasted for approximately four hours. After the graduation ceremony Nathan's father, David, gave a barbecue in the park for Nathan's graduation.

My wife, Derek, Christian, and McKenzie stayed for approximately three hours with Nathan. We informed Nathan that we were very proud of his accomplishment. We drove back to Sacramento, California, and the next day; we took Christian and McKenzie to Marine World for some fun.

The following day we all drove to the Pleasant fair—Gloria, Derek, Christian, McKenzie, Beulah, and I. We stayed at the fair for several hours before returning to Sacramento.

On Thursday June 19, 2013, we drove back to the Oakland airport and caught our flight back to Houston, Texas. We are blessed to have a great-grandson and a grandson graduate from high school in the same year. When I was a child, I had to attend an all-black elementary, junior high, and high school. The school bus that I rode only had black children on board. My grandfather owned a farm, and the entire family worked for him. We were sheltered from a numerous amount of unfair treatment of our people. I remember as a young child going to a retail store with my mother, and she ordered food for us. She was informed that we could not sit down in the store to eat the food. There were signs near the water fountain and bathrooms that read "White Only" and "Colored." When we rode the buses for transportation to the city, we could not sit in the front of the bus. When I was growing up as a child, I could only play with other children that were the same color as I. My school teachers were all African American throughout my entire school years. I worked at a restaurant during my high school years, and I could not enter through the front door. I had to enter through the back door. African Americans that ordered food had to order from the back door. When my mother and I went to stores to shop, we were always followed by a store employee, even to today. I graduated from an all-black high school that had all-black teachers.

When I became of age after we moved to the city, I went to pool halls and restaurants in the city where African American people lived. I remember walking home one night with my cousin and a truck stopped in the street that had four to five white occupants. They were calling us names and thought we were going to run away. We did not run and decided to take them on. They drove away without an incident. I walked home on numerous occasions from the city and was called names as vehicles passed me by. I remember my mother calling a taxi and when she gave the dispatcher our address the taxi never came. We attended a church with all African American members.

During my senior year in high school, some friends and I were asked if we wanted to attend the all-white high school. When I graduated from high school, I attended an all-black junior college. I remember getting on a grey hound bus to attend school and all the seats were full except one seat. The white guy on the seat refused to let me sit down. I could have made him let me sit down and be put off the bus in the middle of the forest and fields.

Years later, I entered the military and received an assignment from North Dakota to Korea. I was informed that once people in the assignment section discovered that I was black they attempted to cancel my assignment. This occurred in 1988, and I had processed out from the base and the assignment could not be cancelled. Once I arrived in Korea there was a commander (06) colonel that contacted my supervisor and asked what qualified me to be in the open mess career field. There were several other noncommissioned officers in the field, and they were not African American. He did not ask if they were qualified to be in the open mess career field. During the time that he was inquiring about my qualification I was enrolled in a master's program on base.

Today some of the major five hundred companies are hiring people from all over the world that do not speak English plainly. They prefer to hire these people than to hire African Americans. We continue to be discriminated against because of the color of our skin and nationality. This practice cannot continue and must stop now. My people need to wake up and be counted.

Today is July 23, 2014, and I am sitting in the waiting room at a hospital, awaiting for my wife to have a procedure performed by her doctor. We have been preparing for our relocation back to Sacramento, California, in September 2014. My wife have began to pack boxes with products, and once the boxes are full, they are taped and stacked in the spare bedroom. The moving trailer will be delivered to our residence on August 29, 2014. Once the trailer is delivered, we have contracted for several loaders to load the heavy furniture and washer and dryer, and we will load the boxes.

We decided to trade our Mercury Mountaineer in on a newer vehicle because it have 132,000 miles on the odometer. The vehicle also requires a numerous amount of work to get it ready to drive cross-country. We visited Sterling McCall Nissan during the month of June in 2014. The salesman showed us three different vehicles: a Dodge Ram Truck, a Toyota Tundra truck, and a Nissan Armanda SUV. The SUV costs less than the two trucks, and we will be able to afford the payments and insurance. We spoke with the finance manager at Sterling McCall Nissan about the vehicle. He informed us to return to the dealership on the end of June 2014 if we wanted to receive the best deal on the vehicle.

We returned to Sterling McCall on June 30, 2014, and we had received financing from a finance company. We had a blank check for $26,000 to purchase a vehicle from any dealership that the finance company approved us to purchase from. When we arrived at the dealership, we met with the salesman and finance manager to inform them that we were interested in purchasing the Nissan Armanda. The salesman and finance manager did not know that we had our financing already. I informed the salesman that I wanted to trade my Mercy Mountaineer in on the SUV, and it must cover the tax and licensing. I also informed him that I did not want to pay any money down on the SUV.

The salesman put several figures together and discussed it with the finance manager and presented them to us. The last deal presented to us required $1,000 down: $1,600 for my vehicle; $24,949 for the SUV; and a monthly payment of $549.

I informed the salesman the we did not require financing because we had our own. Several minutes later the finance manager appeared and asked if we would be interested if he could get us a better deal than the one we had. He explained that the deal included a lower financing percentage, monthly payments would be the same, and the financing period would be the same. The finance manager departed and returned later and informed us that the loan was approved. He processed all the paperwork, and we signed each copy. We were given a copy and the keys to the Armada. We removed all merchandise from the Mountaineer and placed it in the Armada. The following day I returned to the dealership and gave the finance manager the title to the Mountaineer.

We began to receive calls from the finance manager for additional paperwork for proof of income. He was receiving calls from the GM bank personnel. The same day I received a call from the GM bank employee requesting four cancelled checks from my wife's job. I informed her that my wife did not have any cancelled checks because she was paid in cash. We had previously given the finance manager at Sterling McCall pay statements for myself and my wife's job. The next day I received a call from the GM bank employee requesting income verification for me. I gave the employee a name and phone number to call for income verification. The finance manager was receiving calls from the GM bank for approximately two weeks requesting additional paperwork from my wife and I. We received a letter from GM dated July 11, 2014, informing us that they were unable to finance us due to certain reasons. We returned to the dealership with our financing approval and the blank check for $26,000 on July 22, 2014, to finalize the vehicle purchase. We met with the finance manager, and he informed us that the bank manager from GM had visited him at the dealership and stated that he suspected that my wife and I were involved with fraud. We had previously informed the finance manager that my wife had a 1099, and we had our tax forms for the past year. The general manager at the dealership asked the finance manager what was going on with the GM financing.

I had informed my wife that we were receiving the run around from GM because we were black. The finance manager at the dealership informed us that he had informed the GM bank manager that they were racist and did not want to finance us. He also informed him that I was a retired military veteran with twenty-four years of service, and my wife was a senior citizen receiving social security. He also informed the GM manager that we were not the type people to be involved in fraud. We resigned the paperwork at the dealership on July 22, 2014, and gave the finance manager a check for $25,301.90 for the Armada vehicle. I agree with the finance manager when he stated that the GM finance employees are racists. I informed the finance manager if the GM was the last finance company on the earth for me, and when I would be requiring a loan are financing, I would not attempt to get anything from them. I will inform anyone that need a loan or financing not to go to GM for financing.

We were contacted by the finance company on July 24, 2014, and informed that the check for the vehicle must be written for $24,530. The finance company sent a new blank check to me to write for the vehicle. I called the finance manager at the dealership and informed him about the change in the amount of the check. He informed me that the dealership would eat the difference. My wife and I visited the dealership on July 26, 2014, and the finance manager printed new purchase paperwork for the Armada. I filled out the blank check for $24,530 and presented the check to the finance manager. My wife and I drove home, and we were satisfied with the transaction.

I arrived at home on August 1, 2014, and my wife met me as I entered the house. She was holding two letters from the finance company. The letters were printed with information that stated the loan amount that we requested was too high. I called the finance company and spoke to a representative, and he informed me that the letters were generated because the original amount of the check was more than the amount that could be financed. He stated that all financing for the Armada was approved.

We can concentrate on our preparation for our move to Sacramento, California. We have began to search for a home in Sacramento, California, online. Our daughter Gloria and son-in-law and grandson Christian Barker are also searching for homes for us. They live in Sacramento and drive through neighborhoods searching for lease and rent signs at homes. Whenever they locate a home, Gloria send my wife the information on the home and my wife contact the property management office for information on the home. Beulah then arranges a showing of the home with the property management office so Gloria can view the property.

Once Gloria views the property, she e-mails pictures and features of the home to Beulah. Beulah and I review all the information online and decide if the property is for us. Beulah has contacted several property management offices to discuss the availability of different properties. Beulah spoke with a property manager concerning a particular property. The property manager informed my wife that the property was for rent. My wife informed the manager that our son-in-law would contact her and set up an appointment to view the property. The property manager also informed my wife that a $60 deposit was required in order to pick up the key. She stated that the deposit would be returned when the key was returned. When our son-in-law called the property manager to pick up the key, she informed him that the house had been rented.

The following day, Beulah went online and discovered that the house remained available for rent. I informed Beulah that the property manager assumed that she was Caucasian when she spoke to her on the phone. When she discovered that she was African American, she decided to inform her that the home had been rented. My wife located another home, and Gloria, Christian, and Derrick set up an appointment to view the home. She sent pictures, and we were impressed with the pictures. Beulah spoke with the property owner, and we completed an application to lease the property. He informed Beulah that he had to review several applications and would decide the best-qualified applicant. We will continue to search for other homes because the owner my select another applicant.

We continue to prepare for our move to Sacramento, California, in September 2014. Beulah has packed all the boxes with our merchandise. I have began to remove nails from the walls and fill the nail holes. My wife have removed all pictures from the walls and we purchased several wardrobe boxes to place the clothes into. Several days ago we wrapped the couch and chairs, and they are ready to be loaded on to a trailer when the time arrives. We have given our thirty-day notice to our property owner. He informed us that he did not use a realtor any longer to manager his property. He stated that he would process all paperwork dealing with the home. We have been leasing the home for three years. I knew one of my coworkers was searching for a home to lease. I informed him that we would be moving on September 4, 2014, and the home would be available for lease on September 1, 2014. We informed the property owner that we knew a couple that was interested in leasing the home. We gave the property owner the couple's name and phone numbers. They came to the home and performed a walk through and were pleased with the home. The following week the owner and his wife met the couple, and they signed the lease agreement on the home.

I had a carpet cleaner scheduled to come in on September 2, 2014, to shampoo the carpets. My wife and I mowed and edged the yard on Saturday, and we only have one more time to cut and edge the grass. The property owner in California informed us that his sister may sell the house that Beulah found online. We also had our daughter Gloria and son-in-law Derrick and grandson Christian visit the home to see if we liked the home. We completed a rental agreement and submitted it to the landlord. Several days later the property owner called and informed us that we qualified to rent the property. He also informed us to send a security deposit for $1,300 dollars. We purchased a cashier's check for $1,300 and sent it certified to the landlord's sister. My wife have been purchasing moving boxes each day to pack the merchandise into. The moving truck arrived at our home on August 29, 2014, and dropped the trailer so we could load the merchandise. We hired two loaders from the moving company to load the heavy merchandise. My wife and I loaded the boxes and smaller items. We continued to load the truck for three days. The work was hard, and once we began to load the truck, we worked until nightfall.

Finally on September 2, 2014, we completed loading the last piece of merchandise in the moving trailer. The truck driver arrived at twelve thirty to Pick up the trailer, but we were continuing to load it. I had to go purchase some straps to secure the merchandise. The driver ask how long It would take us to complete loading the trailer. I informed him that we would be finished within one hour. The driver hooked the truck to the trailer and drove away from our home at 1:32 p.m. The next project that we faced involved cleaning the home and having it ready for a walk through by the landlord on September 3, 2014. My wife and I began the cleaning process, and she sprayed the oven with oven cleaner and let it set over night. She began to remove the cleaner the next day. I began to wash and clean all the windows inside and outside. After completing the windows, I began to carry trash outside and placed it on the sidewalk for pickup. My wife began to mop the floors, and I began to remove the merchandise from the home and placed it in the vehicle that we were carrying with us.

When the landlord arrived for the walk through, we were in the process of cleaning. The landlord's wife and children accompanied him to the home. They remained at the home for approximately one hour, and they departed. He stated that they would return later to perform the walk through because we were still cleaning. I removed the last nails and filled the remaining nail holes. I unplugged the cable equipment from the television so we could return it to the cable company. Finally we had removed everything from the home, and the landlord returned for the walk through, and we returned the door keys and garage opener to him. We loaded both vehicles with merchandise to transport to California.

My wife and I checked into a hotel for the night. We were within walking distance of several restaurants. Later that night we walked to a restaurant and had dinner. We requested a wake-up call from the hotel receptionist at five the following morning.

We began our drive and stopped for gas and food. We arrived in El Paso, Texas, on September 4, 2014, at 10:15 p.m. We had driven 735 miles, and we checked into the Holiday Inn. We departed El Paso, Texas, on September 5, 2014, at 8:30 p.m. We had 1,197 miles to drive and the drive would take seventeen hours and forty-eight minutes. During the drive we passed through New Mexico, Tucson, and Phoenix Arizona. We arrived in Southern California on September 5, 2014, at 4:30 p.m.

The first gas we purchased in California cost $4.09 per gallon. We were adjusted to paying $3.29, $3.35, and $3.45 per gallon for gas. We knew the gas prices would cost more than the gas in Houston, Texas.

On September 6, 2014, we stayed overnight in Pasadena, California. We departed the following morning at 6:50 am for Sacramento, California. We had to drive 350 miles to arrive in Sacramento, California. We arrived at 1:30 p.m. on September 6, 2014. We drove to the U-Haul company and had my wife's vehicle removed from the trailer and the trailer unhooked from my vehicle. This completed our move from Houston Texas to Sacramento, California.

We met the landlord the following day and signed the paperwork and received the keys. I unloaded the vehicles, and the merchandise was delivered on Friday. My wife have contacted the appropriate agencies to have service provided to the home. This concludes our move from Houston, Texas, to Sacramento, California. Once we arrived in California the moving company contacted us and stated that our furniture was in the warehouse. The furniture was delivered on a Wednesday, and we had three days to unload the trailer. On Saturday my wife and I along with Gloria, our daughter, Derrick her husband and Christian our grandson began to unload the trailer. Derrick's friend also came over to give assistance. I worked inside the trailer moving merchandise to the back part of the trailer. This process made removing the merchandise from the trailer more economical.

During the final stage of unloading, the trailer a box fell on my left ankle causing it to swell and become very sore. On Monday morning I went to the emergency room to have my ankle checked. Once I spoke with a doctor, an x-ray was taken of the ankle. The doctor informed me that I had a fracture, and he could give me crutches to use. I did not want to use crutches, so the nurse placed an ace bandage on my ankle and informed me to keep the ankle elevated. I was also informed to keep my weight off the ankle as much as possible until it healed.

We had our first Thanksgiving dinner with the family on November 27, 2014, in eight years. We had turkey, ham, roast, green beans, corn, dressing, yams, macaroni and cheese, cranberry sauce, collard greens, mashed potatoes, cakes, pies and ice tea. Gloria our daughter made the macaroni and cheese. My wife placed the turkey and roast in the oven early during the morning and they cooked until they were ready. When the roast was removed from the oven it had to cool before it could be sliced. I assisted her in the kitchen as much as possible. When the food was ready to be consumed, the turkey and roast were sliced so each person could serve themselves. My wife and I blessed the food and the family before we began to eat. The other foods were placed on the tables and everyone served themselves. Gloria prepared our grandson Christians plate, who is four years old.

The football game was on, and we could not watch it because our television was not working. My son-in-law, Derrick, removed a television from the bedroom and placed it in the family room. We ran a cable from the bedroom to the family room and connected it to the television. My sixteen grandson Isaiah was there with his father Clifford. His dad was busy changing his diaper and feeding him. We had a good Thanksgiving dinner with the family members and look forward to many more.

I began my job search after we had everything settled in the home. I went online and also attended a job fair. I gave several companies a resume. I made contact with three security representatives. I did not possess a guard card at the time and could not be hired until I possessed a card. I went online and completed all the requirements for the first eight hours to obtain a guard card. I paid $34 to the state for the license and $64 for fingerprinting and a background check.

Before moving to Sacramento, California, I was employed with ABM security in Houston, Texas. I was informed by the manager in Houston that I could transfer from Houston to California. When I visited the Sacramento security branch, I was informed that I had to start over and complete the paperwork as a new hire. After I completed the paperwork, I interviewed with the captain and lieutenant for a security position. I explained to them that I wanted to work Mondays through Fridays with the weekends off. I also wanted to work forty hours per week. I was informed that I had to work into a Mondays through Fridays shift, and I could not be guaranteed forty hours per week. I was placed on a ninety-day probation because I was starting at a new location. The following week I was also hired by a different security company. The company offered two days of classes to fulfill the guard card requirement. I attended the two-day class for eight hours per day. I was offered a post with the company that paid $9.50 per hour. I did not accept the post because the pay was too low. The following week I was offered .50 more per hour at a post with the first company. I accepted the offer and began to train at two different posts.

I began to train for several days. Later I began working Mondays through Wednesdays from 1:00 p.m. to 9: 00 p.m. and Thursdays through Fridays from 4:00 p.m. to midnight.

Today is December 2014 and my ankle is 95 percent healed. On December 19, 2014, at noon I am sitting in my vehicle watching truck drivers deliver empty trailers to the lot. The rain is coming down, and I do not plan to go outside until my shift ends. When the truck drivers enter the lot to pick up trailers and they work for a different company, I am required to ask for their driver's license and annotate my paperwork, showing the name of their trailer they are picking up and the name of their trucking company.

I work on this site two days per week from 4:00 a.m. to twelve noon and at a different site from 1:00 p.m. to 9:00 p.m. Mondays to Wednesdays. The reason that I am working for this company is that I was offered more money than the previous company. I have been working for this company for approximately two weeks. I also work on some Saturdays from 4:00 p.m. to 11:00 p.m. I received one paycheck from the company, and I received a call from the scheduler with the previous company. He informed me that he had a post open at a library that paid $9.50 per hour. I declined to take the post because the pay was not high enough.

Several weeks later he called again stating that he had an opening at a different site that paid more than the company that I was employed with. My schedule would be Saturdays to Wednesdays with Thursdays and Fridays off. I informed him that I would visit the site on Saturday and inform him if I was interested. After visiting the site, I contacted the scheduler and informed him that I would work at the site. My job involves signing in visitors and contractors to the site. I also open the gate for residents when they do not have their gate opener. The guard shack is at a gated community for homes ranging from $500,000 and above. The residents are very nice and always wave and say hello when they enter and leave the property. I think I will remain at this site until I obtain employment in a different category.

I called the previous company and informed the lieutenant that I was resigning because I had a better-paying job. I had all the uniforms from the previous company cleaned and returned them to the company.

My wife and I completed our Christmas shopping today. She stated that she wanted a name brand purse that cost approximately $350 for Christmas. When we were in the store shopping, she informed me that she hope that I did not buy her a present because she wanted the purse. I purchased three different gifts for her and wrapped them when we arrived home. I placed the presents under the tree so she could open them on Christmas Day.

On Christmas Day we had family members over for dinner and gifts. She had begun to cook the dinner a day before Christmas and completed everything Christmas morning. When the family members arrived, we gave them their gifts, and we sat down for dinner. Some of the gifts were delivered to our son and grandson Christmas night. Our granddaughter received her gift on the day after Christmas. I drove my wife over to deliver her Christmas gift.

I am now concentrating on getting a state, county, or city job. My energy will be geared to those areas to pursue a new career. This year is coming to a close, and I hope that I have a new job starting in 2015. We also fried a turkey in the turkey fryer for Christmas dinner.

Today is December 27, 2014, and I am back at work from 9:30 a.m. to 5:30 p.m. I have not received many visitors today. The majority of the people arriving at the gate have been residents. I have had only one contractor that arrived at the gate. The site is located in Lincoln, California. We live approximately twenty-five minutes driving time from the site. When we lived in California eight years ago, I worked in Lincoln at a different site. I use the same freeway to come to work and go home as I used before. I will continue to work here until I find a better-paying job.

My wife and I plan to move within ten months. We plan to purchase a home so we will not be paying someone's mortgage. I have began to search for homes on the Internet. I am also searching for homes in a upscale community depending on the price range of the homes. We are searching for a four-bedroom home with two bathrooms, a family room with at least 1,900 square feet. I do not want to live close to the city. We plan to live outside the city limits. My wife do not want to live too far from the city. We must live within driving distance of the city because we must pick up our grandson Christian from school. We have seen people living in all types of communities, and we plan to live in a good community.

We do not care about the nationality of the people living in the community. We will not live in a community where the residents do not work. The residents in the community must have some type of income to support themselves, such as social security or retirement.

When my wife and I returned to California, the drought had been there for several years before our arrival. I can water the lawn for fifteen minutes on Tuesdays and Saturdays. The vehicles can be washed in the driveway provided that the waterhose have a shutoff water sprayer. Most homes do not have lawns due to the drought. The back lawn is 95 percent brown, and the front lawn is 30 percent brown. Some people are replacing their lawns with bark and mulch. We take shorter showers and baths. We do not let the water run when we brush our teeth. When I shave each day, I do not let the water run continuously. After each stroke of the razor, I turn the water on to clean the razor. We fill the dishwasher with dishes and wash the dishes once per week.

We purchase bottle water versus faucet water. We do not use the sprinkler system because it use too much water. We are performing procedures to use less water to eliminate the drought condition.

My last day working was 2 July 2021. Prior to my last day working I worked for a company reliving officers for lunch and regular breaks. There were two officers in three different buildings. The numbers changed later to three officers in each building. Because of the locations of the buildings and post I walked several miles each time to give breaks. I had to eat lunch at a post while giving a break to an officer. I began to give breaks to the lobby officer in building one. The second break was given to the officer in the special unit. I drove to building two to begin the second breaks. The lobby officer received the first break. The second break was given to the officer at the special unit. Next, I went to building three to give the lobby officer a break. Then I went to the cage to give the officer a break. Each officer received two ten- minute breaks and a thirty- minute lunch break during their shift. One lobby officer was added in each building, and I had to also give those officers two ten- minute breaks and one thirty- minute lunch break.

My left hip had began to hurt each time I walked. I went to my family practice doctor and was referred to the orthopedic doctor. When I arrived at the hospital, I went to the wheelchair area and my wife pushed me in a wheelchair to the orthopedic lobby, where I checked in. I went to the orthopedic doctor's office and explained to her about my hip. She sent me to the x-ray area to have an x-ray taken. The next day I received a call that I must return to the doctor to discuss my hip injury. When I arrived, the orthopedic doctor informed me that I had a hip fracture. The doctor informed me that I could have surgery to correct the fracture. She also informed me that I could let the hip heal naturally. I informed the doctor that I wanted to let the hip heal naturally. She also prescribed some 500mg pills to use when I could not stand the pain. I took the pills one time during my healing process. I was also given a shot within a two-year time frame for pain. I was given a cane and a walker to use the healing process. The scheduling department scheduled me to return to see the doctor every three months. The doctor scheduled me to get an x-ray before some appointments so she could look at the x-ray to see how the hip was healing. This process continued for two years. The doctor gave me a unable to work form to give my employer each time I was scheduled to see her. Finally, the doctor reviewed an x-ray that showed my hip was healing naturally. The doctor informed me that I had permanent arthritis in my left hip. I continue to have pain in my hip. I take Tylenol for arthritis for the pain. When I am walking and place weight on my left foot, I feel the pain in my left hip.

One additional officer was added to assist me with the ten minute and lunch breaks. The second officer started his shift at 10am. I ended my shift at 4pm Monday thru Friday. I continue to be in pain every day.

Book Summary

This book lists the place where William Hodge was born, which is Axton, Virginia. Some of the homes that William and his family lived in did not have windows. William's father covered the openings with plastic to prevent the wind and cold air from entering the home. Some of the homes had roof leaks and pans were placed on the floor to catch the rain water.

When William began school, he attended Irshburg Elementary School, Leatherwood Elementary, East Martinsville Junior High, George Washington Carver High, and Albert Harris High School, where he graduated in June 1967. After graduating from high school, William attended Kittrell College for one and one half years. William did not plan to attend college after graduating from high school. One of his former coaches called him and asked if he wanted to attend college. He also informed him to be ready to leave for school within one week after speaking with him. William contacted the coach one week after speaking with him and stated he wanted to attend college. The coach contacted the dean of admission and arranged for William to take the college entrance examination once he arrived on campus. When William was ready to leave Martinsville, Virginia to attend college, his mother and father accompanied him to the Greyhound bus station. They purchased a bus ticket for William, and he said his goodbyes. William had never been away from home before. His mother had to become adjusted to him being away from home.

When William arrived at Kittrell College, he was given the college entrance examination and placed on the work-study program. The money William earned from the work-study program was used to pay the school cost. William was issued a student deferment during the time he was in school. He could not get drafted into the military while he was in school. William decided to return home and search for employment after attending school for one year. William applied for employment at a textile manufacturing plant and was hired. After working for approximately three months William was reclassified as 1A, and he was eligible to get drafted.

William did not want to go to Vietnam if he was drafted, so he contacted an air force recruiter. He decided that the air force was the best way to go. The air force recruiter scheduled William for a battery of tests to determine the area he was best qualified to apply for. When the test results came back, William was qualified for the information management career field. He was scheduled to take a physical in Roanoke, Virginia, where he stayed overnight. When the results from the examination was received, William was sworn in and placed on a delayed enlistment program for several months. William continued to work at the plant until he entered the military. When an opening came available, William went to Roanoke, Virginia, and was flown to Lackland Air Force Base in Texas for eight weeks of basic training. After completing basic training William was placed on a bus and sent to Keesler Air Force base in Biloxi Mississippi, to attend the information management school.

Hurricane Camille hit the Gulf Coast and destroyed the area. The school was closed for several months and all students were placed on details. The details consisted of area clean up, issuing food, water and clothing to the civilian population. After several months the school reopened and William graduated and received an assignment to Travis Air Force base in Fairfield, California. William was assigned to the forms and publication section in the Combat Support Group. He was sent to Vietnam after being assigned to Travis Air Force Base for one year.

William and Beulah continued to date and were married on October 17, 1973. They traveled to different military bases in the states and overseas during his military career. William retired from the United States Air Force on June 1, 1993, after serving for twenty-four years.

Gloria Barker

Derrick Barker

Christian T. Barker

Beulah Hodge—wife

William Hodge

Glora Barker—daughter

Derrick Barker—son-in-law

Christian T. Barker—15th grandson

Christian T. Barker—15th grandson

William Hodge receives an award

William Hodge on tour in Turkey

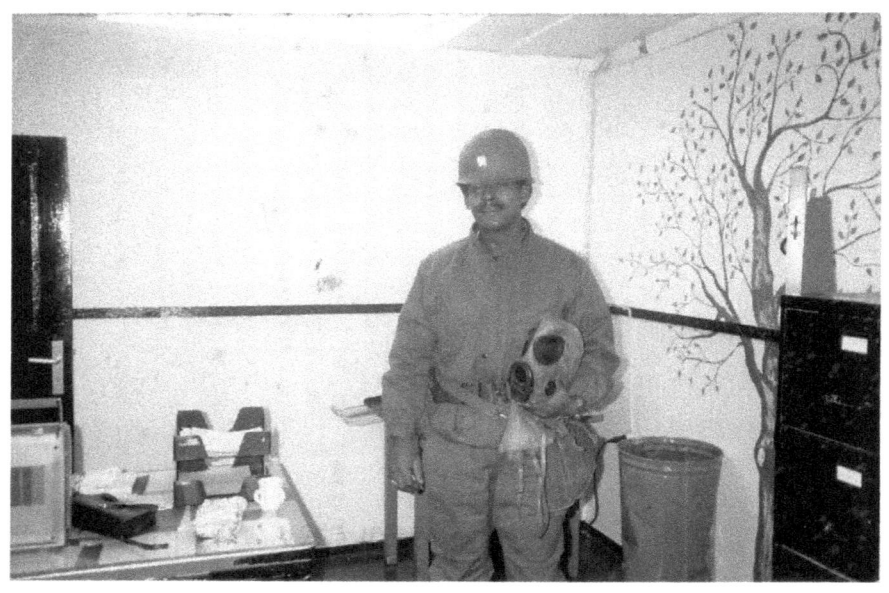

William Hodge on tour in Germany

William Hodge a member of the Masonic Lodge

THE ALBERT HARRIS YELLOW JACKETS;
STRONG AND ALMIGHTY.

VIA   COACHES   PRITCHETT

COACH HAIRSTON   COACH EDWARDS   COACH WYLIE

1966   BASKETBALL TEAM   1967

William Hodge on backrow third from the left

William Hodge—graduated high school at Albert Harris
High School

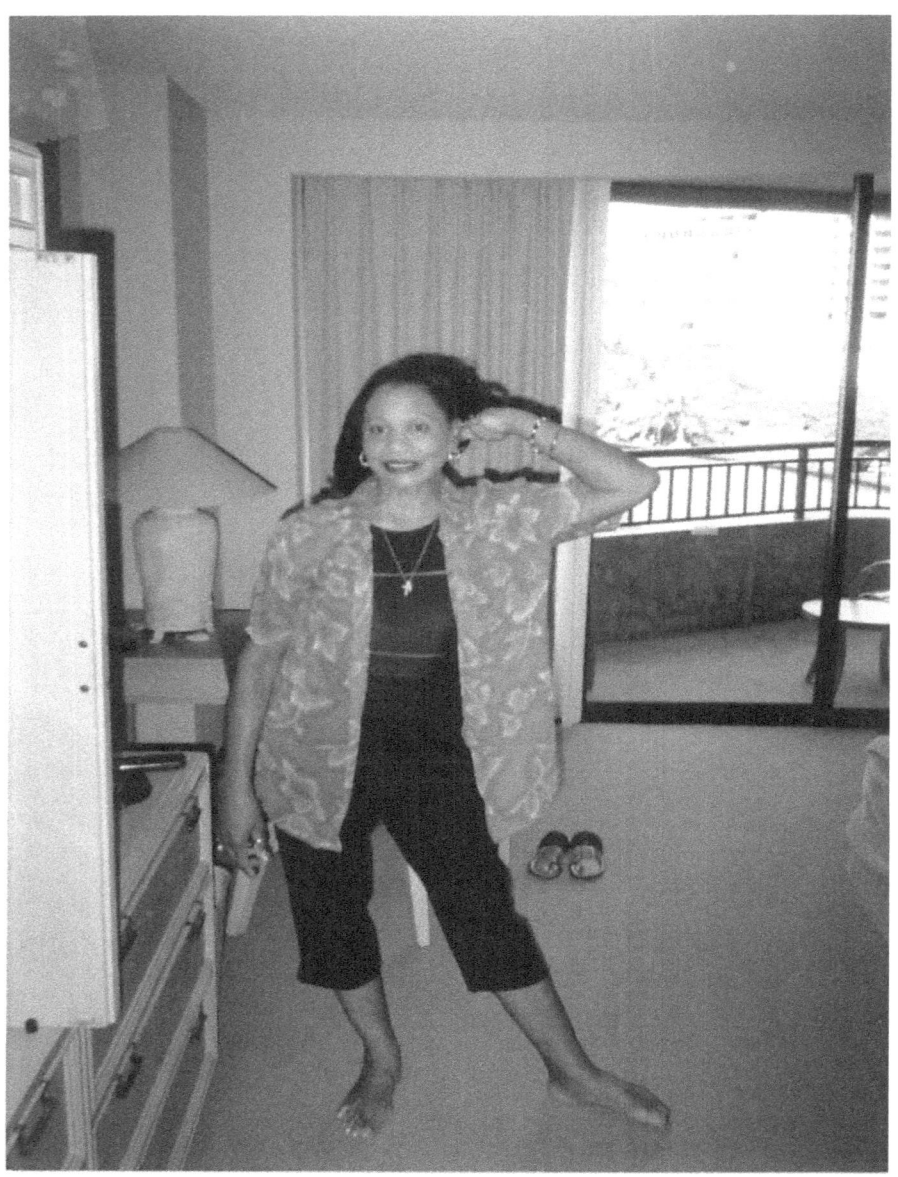

My wife Beulah Hodge

William Hodge on tour in South Vietnam,
William is the guy wearing the sun shades.
Myron Webb is friend sitting in the middle.
Gwen is friend on the left.

Makita Lucas, granddaughter,
Ernest Lucas, her husband

William Hodge received the Master of Arts
degree from the University of Phoenix.

Camella T. Hodge—Granddaughter

Tavio McAllister—Grandson

Te'von Rhyne—Tavio's brother

Makenzee McAllister—Granddaughter

Patricia Osemwingie—Our daughter

Isaiah Osemwingie—Her son

Noah Osemwingie—Her son

Martina Osemwingie—Her daughter

Carmell Taylor Hodge—Her daugter

Our son Clifford McAllister
Tavio McAllister our grandson and our granddaughter

My grandson Josh McAllister with his brother Nathan McAllister after high school graduation. They are accompanied by their grandmother Beulah Hodge

William Hodge receives an award

Left - Beulah Hodge, my wife, next - William Hodge, Gloria
Barker, our daughter and Derrick Barker our son-in-law

REFERENCES

WWW.davidhowardemery.com/?category_name=air force-basic training En.wikipedia.org/wiki/Keesler_AFB www.travis.af.mil/ news/ story.asp?id=123269572 en.wikipedia.org/wiki/Tan_Son_ Nhut_ Air_Base en.wikipedia.org/wiki/Homestead_Air_Force_Base Izmir Turkey En.wikipedia/Wikipedia.org/wiki/Beale_Air_Forve_ Base En.wikipedia.org/qwiki/Spangdahlem_Air_Base En.wikipedia. org/ wiki/Holloman_Air_Base_ en.wikipedia.org/wiki/Tan_Son_ Nhut_ Air_Base en.wikipedia.org/wiki/Osan_Air_Base en.wikipedia.org/wiki/ Hurricane_Camille www.grandforks.af.mil http//civil-rights.findlaw. com/otherconstitutional-rig.

ABOUT THE AUTHOR

William Hodge was born 4 October 1948 in Axton Virginia. He attended Irshburg and leatherwood elementary schools. William had eight brothers and two sisters. He attended Albert Harris High School and was active in football and track. William attended Kittrell College for one and one half years. He entered the United States Air Force on 29 May 1969. The first assignment was at Travis Air Force Base in California. He met his wife Beulah in Oakland California in 1970. They were married on 17 October 1973 and have five children, sixteen grandchildren and eleven great grandchildren. William received an Associate of Arts degree from Thomas Edison College, he received a Bachelor of Science degree on 4 December 1984 from Troy State University. William retired from the United States Air Force on 1 June 1993 after serving for twenty-four years. He received a Master of Arts degree on 31 March 2003 from the University of Phoenix. William enjoys sports and going to a good movie with his wife and eating popcorn. William is a born again believer and attends Bayside church in midtown in Sacramento California. William enjoys growing his beard when he is off work so his wife can say "you need to shave". He enjoys taking his wife out for dinner to eat seafood or a good steak. He enjoys having dinner with the family members on holidays or whenever they drop in unannounced. William and his wife Beulah attempt to spend as much time together as possible. They normally go fishing together and shop in the malls. William enjoys wearing fancy suits when going to specific places and surprising his wife Beulah with special gifts on her birthdays. William enjoys working on projects that will generate income for him in the future. He developed a new pizza sauce and pizza. William has not placed the items on the market for sale. William enjoys treating his fellow man with love and respect.

When my wife and I were planning our 50th wedding ceremony, we decided to purchase new rings. We went to a jewelry store and selected rings for each of us. We had our fingers sized and the rings were sent out. The rings were out for two weeks before they were returned to the store. The salesperson contacted us to come into the store to see if the rings fit properly. When we arrived at the store, we met the salesperson and the rings fit perfectly and we were happy. We had not purchased rings for fifty years. In the beginning I was not planning to purchase a ring for myself. My wife insisted that I get a ring. Happy wife, Happy life. I asked my grandson Tavio McAllister to be my best man. Our daughter Gloria Barker was my wife's maid of honor. My other grandson Christian Barker would escort my wife into the chapel. We called the Mon Bel Ami Wedding chapel in Las Vegas and set everything up for the wedding. My grandsons and my wife and I went to the tuxedo shop to select suit styles and colors. Once the styles were selected, we were measured for the tuxedos. The tuxedos arrived at the tuxedo shop after two weeks and we went to the shop and tried everything for a fit. My wife called the Circus Circus hotel and Casino in Las Vegas and made reservation for our stay. My wife made reservation with the airlines for our flight to Las Vegas one day prior to our ceremony. We also made reservations for a rental van in Las Vegas. We drove to the Sacramento airport for our flight to Las Vegas. Once we arrived in Las Vegas we picked-up the van and drove to the Circus Circus hotel. When we arrived at the hotel there were so many people in the hotel lobby that we could not check in. We decided to return to the hotel later in the evening to check-in. We decided to go to dinner prior to checking into the hotel. When we returned to the hotel the lines of people had gone. After we checked in my wife and I and her niece went to see the Michael Jackson One show in another hotel. We arose early in the morning and ate breakfast and prepared for our ceremony. When the time was drawing close, I checked my grandsons' ties and suits to ensure that everything looked good. My wife and I and our daughter Gloria and Derrick Barker, her niece and husband departed the hotel to wait for the limousine to arrive. The limousine driver arrived at the hotel and drove us to the chapel. When we arrived at the chapel there were other ceremonies in progress. The Pastor came out and informed My wife and I to enter the chapel. He informed us how the ceremony would proceed. I was informed to enter the area where the ceremony would take place. I would stand at the podium on the left side. My grandson Christian Barker escorted my wife into the chapel, and she stood beside me. Tavio McAllister escorted Gloria Barker, the maid of honor into the chapel. Family members that were not part of the ceremony were seated. The ceremony began and I attempted to read my vows to my wife. I could not hold the tears back. My wife said her vows and we lit the candles. My wife and I placed the rings on each other's finger. We departed the chapel to take pictures in the outside entry area of the chapel. The limousine driver returned to drive us back to the hotel. After changing clothes, we drove to a restaurant for dinner. We then returned to the hotel and packed our suitcases for a return home. The next morning, we drove to the airport and boarded the plane for our trip home.